City Beautiful"

ORO Editions
Publishers of Architecture, Art, and Design
Gordon Goff: Publisher

www.oroeditions.com
info@oroeditions.com

Published by ORO Editions
Copyright © 2022 Christian Bjone.

Author: Christian Bjone
Book Design: T.R. Nimen
Project Coordinator: Alejandro Guzman-Avila, Kirby Anderson
Managing Editor: Jake Anderson

10 9 8 7 6 5 4 3 2 1 First Edition

ISBN: 978-1-954081-69-7
Color Separations and Printing: ORO Group Ltd.
Printed in China.

ORO Editions makes a continuous effort to minimize the overall carbon footprint of
its publications. As part of this goal, ORO Editions, in association with Global ReLeaf,
arranges to plant trees to replace those used in the manufacturing of the paper
produced for its books. Global ReLeaf is an international campaign run by American
Forests, one of the world's oldest nonprofit conservation organizations. Global
ReLeaf is American Forests' education and action program that helps individuals,
organizations, agencies, and corporations improve the local and global environment
by planting and caring for trees.

This book is dedicated to my sister, Linda,
who knows Chicago far better than I.

I LOVE CHICAGO'S BUILDINGS

A SELECTIVE GUIDE TO THE CITY

CHRISTIAN BJONE

TABLE OF CONTENTS

Introduction

I grew up in a classic Bungalow type house on the far west side of Chicago, right at the border line. At the fair age of seven my very paranoid parents forced me to memorize my home address, in a sing-song voice, "1630 North Nagle, Chicago Illinois" in the case of being lost, kidnapped, hit by a bus or an unauthorized escape to adventure with pirates on the high seas (the last was a short-lived attempt only once). That address remains tattooed in my brain even if that time was long ago and I live so far away.

Today, I am an architect, designer, author and this book is a very personal interpretation and very eccentric selection of buildings in my Chicago that I love. Your Chicago will be most different and maybe even more coherent, but mine remains the most knowledgeable listing that was made by a small child riding on his bike (the Schwinn "Panther" model) block after block. The perceptions and understanding of that young boy were quite amazing.

In a time of perilous plague travel, this book is written far from Chicago and is a stroll in my mind's-eye; re-assembling each door, window, building and block, a similar act of imagination to what Joyce did for Dublin and Dante did for Hell.

This is not a typical guide book nor a generic history tale and not even a disguised autobiography. It is a listing of select pairs of buildings that each articulates a formal and abstract concept that is part of the culture of Architecture, spelled with a capital A. The main idea of the book is to hide the bitter pill of academic formal analysis in a dollop of sugary personal anecdotes and humor. Hopefully, this will be creating unexpected juxtapositions that might elicit shock and new perceptions, canceling the sleepy accepted dogma we all live under. I will be pairing the famous and the infamous, the profound and the absurd, the beloved and the forgotten, the monstrous and the minuscule.

The book is organized into five sections in a rough chronological order that accepts mixing and matching of dates and styles of various buildings. The sequence is Old Modern (usually labeled as Early Modern), New Modern, Post Modern, Future Modern (I invented this label) and the Conclusion.

The original objective was to have each of the paired objects located nearby in a walkable distance to make the comparisons more immediate. That did not work out at all. And so you are now forced (dear hypercritical reader, my likeness, my brother) to either give up on the challenge and stay reading at home or use the book as a pocket reference to consult on those long walks that Chicago demands.

Or on any bicycle journey that is your personal escape to adventure on the high seas and beyond.

Christian Bjone
New York City during COVID-19, plague lock down
November 1, 2020

OLD MODERN

LOCKED DOORS AND HIDDEN TREASURES

MIES, SULLIVAN AND THE COSMOS

The first essay takes on the theme of "Fragments," this is a code word in Architect-Speak (I invented this word) that covers some contradictory ground. To put it simply, it is the incomplete piece or part of a building that contains the DNA of the larger structure. And so we take the object of the "door" and see how small and obvious an element of a building can take on a monumental importance, if you do a close reading of it. The three doors, which we will pry open to find their secrets, are a main entry door to an apartment building—historical fragment, then an elevator door to a demolished office building—mechanical fragment and lastly an entry door to a historic science museum—scientific fragment.

ENTRY ARCH—200 EAST PEARSON STREET

The main entry door to the apartment building at 200 East Pearson Street seems quite innocuous but it has a few secrets to discover. The building designed, by architect Robert DeGolyer in 1917, seems like any upscale apartment blocks of the period: mostly masonry, double hung windows, a little bit of neoclassical ornament and a cheapo cornice at the top. The entry doors are surrounded by an ornamental fake rustication set of blocks to give a little class to the front door. But to look closer you can see the blocks are not even stone, they are cast concrete with smooth pebble aggregates. And here is the first secret of the door: it is a one third size version of the monumental stone entry arch at the Palazzo Farnese in Rome, Italy (1550+). The original had to be big enough to drive a horse and carriage through to the courtyard beyond. Yes, the monumental Italian Renaissance has been brought to Chicago, but in microscopic size. It even copies the fleur-de-lys ornament in the top band reminding us of the many fake Medici's that live within.

The second secret of the door is that this was once the home to the great German/American modern architect Ludwig Mies van der Rohe. Please note the nearby westward street is ceremoniously titled Mies van der Rohe Way. Instead of living in his amazing modern floor to ceiling glass apartment buildings, 860/880 N. Lake Shore Drive, built close by, he resided in an example of very bourgeois, traditional housing. I have been told that his unit was on the second floor facing west and south. Was this an element of hypocrisy of the master builder commanding: live as I say, not as I do? Or is it a more complicated reality: here is an old guy who fled Germany in his mid-fifties, who was never comfortable with English and didn't want to be bothered by his neighbor's plumbing problems in a Mies-designed building. Also it gives us the door as a historical fragment of both an imagined Renaissance glory and, for Mies, the safety of a symbol of European culture under attack in Crass Capitalist America. Maybe it even can be seen as part of a complex urban collage, that Mies was so fond of making, which pushes the entry arch together, in our mind, with Mies' collection of Kurt Schwitters collage artwork displayed in his dining room (as guests at his dining room table?) to make everything we see a fragment of something else.

ELEVATOR DOOR—CHICAGO STOCK EXCHANGE

Louis Sullivan was an amazing genius of the 1890s "Chicago School," whose ornament we will talk about later, but there was something strange about his elaborate proto-art nouveau ornament designs that were applied to any surface material—metal, wood, tile, terracotta without any adjustment to the qualities of those materials. As his student, Frank Lloyd Wright, would remark in the book *Genius and the Mobocracy*: "The Master would apply his art to any material but was the best in the ways of terracotta." So it is quite a surprise to see the design of the elevator door to his long gone building, the Chicago Stock Exchange (1894), mounted on a wall in the upper level of the Art Institute of Chicago's main entry stair hall, manufactured in a way that contradicts all the other ornament that Sullivan produced. If the normal procedure is for Sullivan to produce his elaborate geometric/floral ornament in pencil and then force it into whatever material was at hand, this elevator door thing is entirely different. Just a side note, he pronounced his first name with a pretentious French inflection as "Lu-we" and not the bland Louis.

The ornament is a grid of concentric circles made of curved narrow bands of metal that are connected by metal spindles and elaborated at its center by metal spheres on brackets. The point being that the ornament is made directly from the materials and attachment process and not just imposed from above. So here we have a presumed Sullivan ornament that has no relation to any other Sullivan ornament. This is made obvious in another Sullivan elevator door, located in the Los Angeles County Museum of Art (LACMA) that has a larger piece of the elevator cage. Here the typical cast metal Sullivan pattern is directly above the doors in question. The secret of this Sullivan door is who the hell designed this thing that is obviously not by Sullivan.

Frank Lloyd Wright may have been employed in the Adler & Sullivan office during the design of this object (he was fired in 1893 while the building was in design) but it seems hard to believe that such a monstrous ego would not have claimed responsibility for such a dramatic design. But another connection in favor of Wright was that the metal work was manufactured by Winslow Brothers Co., the clients of one of Wright's first houses, which we will visit in the next essay.

The door is a hypnotically beautiful pattern of curved lines and dots made in metal, but it is also an object that stands outside of its context, being a modern construction of art that surpasses the ideas of the moment it was made and becomes something more modern than the word was defined at its conception. An abstract modern sculpture at home in the 2000s as much as the 1900s. I passionately believe it is simply the best of its time, disguised under an incorrect label and hiding the true name of its maker. Another door with its silent secrets.

Note: There are other "birdcage" elevator enclosures from the same period that still exist (but as ornament only) as in the Reliance Building (1895), now the Hotel Burnham.

ENTRY DOOR — ADLER PLANETARIUM

The Adler Planetarium was opened in 1929, at the start of such despair in this country that the building is both an unaffordable extravagance and an inspiration of hope and joy. That is how I always thought of this building. With its romantic location of being isolated at the edge of the lake, its rich color and texture of polished red/brown granite, its severe geometry of twelve-sided base and copper-clad spherical dome, and its exquisite art deco ornamental panels of the zodiac. It is an other-worldly object that contains other-worldly objects. I don't know why people don't love this building as much as I do.

    The main entry doors are especially delightful for children (or childish architects). Because the doors are set in a bright bronze-clad grid holding a set of thick beveled glass panels that act as prisms, which on sunny days can diffract the light and cast rainbow patterns on the floor and walls of the entry vestibule. Architecture can't give more unexpected joy than this. The entry vestibule is clad in more polished granite panels with a circular dedication plaque surrounded by bas-relief sculpture of eight Roman gods who represent the eight planets in our solar system, by the artist Alfonso Iannelli. That seems to give a fairy tale quality to the room.

Please note that Pluto (the fake ninth planet) was yet to be discovered at the time of construction and since then has been divorced from the solar system family being labeled as no more than a dumb rock with pretensions.

    The design of the door with beveled glass edges can be seen as a little kitsch, a little crazy and a lot of fun. But because they relate to the scientific theme of the building they are totally reasonable. What is the secret of this door? So few Chicago Architects know that it exists.

Note: With the new addition to the museum there is a new ground level main entry, so the old doors at the top of the steps are locked and closed, in order to experience the rainbows you must enter below and walk up to the original entry vestibule.

Doorknob and doorplate, cast iron
Chicago Stock Exchange (1894)
Designer: Louis Sullivan

200 E. Pearson St. (1917)
Architect: Robert DeGolyer
The residence of the modern architect
Ludwig Mies van der Rohe
during 1950–1969

Entry arch and door at the Palazzo Farnese at Rome, Italy (1550+)
Architect: Antonio da Sangallo and later Michelangelo

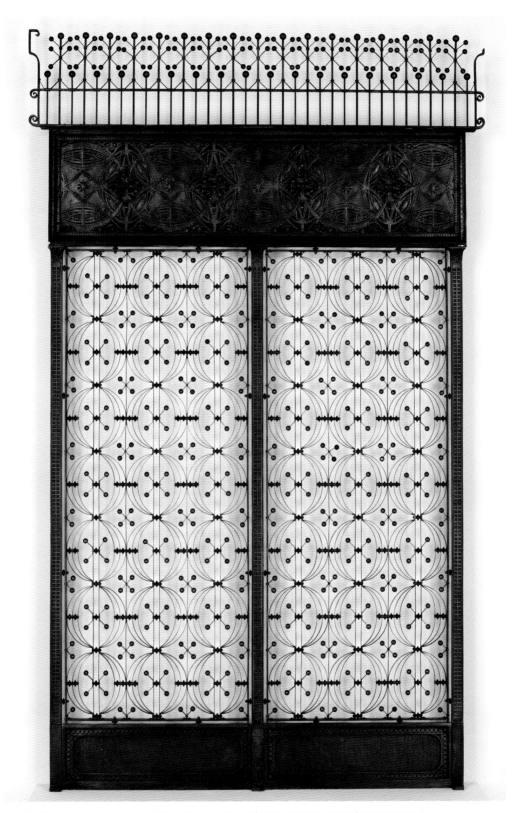

Louis Sullivan elevator cage for the Chicago Stock Exchange (1894, demolished 1972) with cast metal ornamental lintel at the Los Angeles County Museum of Art (LACMA). The pair of doors exist as a sculpture on the wall of the central stair atrium at the Art Institute of Chicago.

Adler Planetarium (1930) - 1300 S. Lake Shore Dr. - Architect: Ernest Grunsfeld - Addition (1999) Architect: Lohan Assoc.

Right: Art deco entry door at the
Adler Planetarium with thick
beveled glass window panes.

MENTOR AND STUDENT

LOUIS SULLIVAN AND FRANK LLOYD WRIGHT

Frank Lloyd Wright is the most famous architect son of the city of Chicago, although he would argue about his allegiance to any city. However, his education as a professional architect would most evidently start in Chicago at 1887 when hired by the firm of Adler & Sullivan (and fired in 1893) with his employer and mentor the great architect Louis Sullivan. But who was Louis Sullivan? Sullivan has been called "the Father of the Skyscraper," which does not mean he did the first skyscraper (or the tallest of his time) but that he defined it in his essay *The Tall Building Artistically Considered* and early work like the Wainwright Building (1890) in St. Louis, a clear and simple composition that expressed the vertical nature of the structure. Also, another invention of Sullivan is his own form of ornament in a combination of hard geometry and curved line. He is America's giant of art nouveau design, alongside Louis Comfort Tiffany.

These two buildings, Charnley House (1892) in the city and Winslow House (1894) in the suburbs, show the interaction between the two men at the end of their professional friendship.

Apprenticeship in architecture is a double-edged sword. To learn, the student has to submit to the ideas of the teacher and then he must ignore those lessons to become true to his own values and vision.

It is generally agreed that Wright worked on the Charnley house but Sullivan was the designer in control. What was built was a four-story urban townhouse, a solid cube of orange masonry, a razor thin copper cornice, a heavy 7-foot tall limestone base, strict symmetry, a planar simplicity that is enlivened by the central second floor loggia and its delicate linear ornament cut out of the wood panels. It is a facade with a singular voice and style that was unlike anything in the city. Bravo!

And then two years later we have one of Wright's first independent houses completed. The linage from Charnley to Winslow is obvious. The sold cube of orange masonry is still there but now it weighted down by a large hip roof. The primary shaped square windows are still there but now they are big bright eyes in the buildings face. The symmetry is still there but the second floor is now become a horizontal band of brown terracotta ornament that collects and hides the bedroom windows on that floor. The ornament now surrounds the limestone entry; another thin line. It is not one of the many prairie school houses that Wright would later produce but something all its own. He takes the basic elements of Charnley and bends them to slightly different qualities. Applause!

They are related, but neither brother nor sister, something else entirely. Perhaps they are one schizoid person with two different colored eyes (heterochromia) that each views a different world. Or maybe they are bookends to a moment that neither architect continued as both were moving in opposite directions. Similar and yet so different.

I look upon them in wonder.

The Charnley House (1892) - 1365 N. Astor St., Chicago - Architect: Louis Sullivan

The Winslow House (1894) - 515 Auvergne Pl., River Forest - Architect: Frank Lloyd Wright

ORNAMENT AS DELIGHTFUL SCHIZOPHRENIA

LOUIS SULLIVAN AND THOMAS BEEBY

SCHIZ-O-PHREN-IA —Defined in general use as a mental attitude characterized in the belief of contradictory elements.

There is in some of the 1890s Chicago School's most famous high-rise buildings a structural clarity, order and rigor that is the admiration of the world of design while at the same time overlapping with a separate ornamental exuberance, sensuality and disorder that appears to contradict the first system.

Fred Nietzsche would have characterized this as the simple contrast of cultural orders: the Apollonian golden order and clarity with its twin opposite the Dionysian dark and chaotic subconscious.

Obviously this doesn't bother the architects noted in this essay and most other people in the world, but it drives me C-R-A-Z-Y!

There is an essay from the late historian, Colin Rowe, titled *The Chicago Frame* (1956) that chastises the turn of the last century's Chicago architects for their limited view on the artistry of the steel frame and tries to explain this by saying it is all capitalism's fault. Rowe noted that "...it was considered aesthetically desirable that the frame be modified, this process was rationalized in terms of the need for psychological expressiveness in the facade rather than in any need for internal spatial excitement." I believe that the phrase "the psychological expressiveness in the facade" is the most charming way of calling out both the structure and the ornament of Sullivan.

The business center of the city (later called the Loop) was a constricted area limited by the river on the north and west, the stockyards on the south and the lakefront park on the east. So the skyscraper evolved from the purely economic forces, built upward for profit on the limited business area with the lot sizes available. But the cheapest possible structure did not have the cultural status for marketing as the sole image of a prestigious office building. Hence you have the schizophrenia of two cultural forces existing at the same place and time. Somewhat like the cultural remnants of sweet Victorian sentimentality aligned with its ruthless, exploitive imperialism. The combination did not bother Queen Victoria at all.

SULLIVAN AND DESIGN SCHIZOPHRENIA

Louis Sullivan was a genius in the production of an American Art Nouveau architectural ornament. The geometric vegetation drawn from his pencil covered almost everything: not just facades and column capitals but wallpaper, doorknobs, stair railings and elevator grilles. I have chosen the beloved hulk of a former department store: the Carson Pirie Scott & Co. building (1892) to represent this attitude but also a strange gesture of compromise to the schizophrenia. Because in this building you get not only the tangle of intertwined bronze vines, leaves and flourishes at the ground floor entries and shop windows but something unexpected and stranger on the floors above. The relentless structural grid of the plan is reflected

19

up on the facade in the same clarity and simplicity with the most refined and subtle traced lines of decoration. If you look closely you can see that the inside edges of the white rectangular terracotta window frames have discrete thin bands of filigree. So the building presents itself with the schizophrenia of a wild jungle of embellishment below and a tended garden of ornamental vines above.

You could say that Sullivan used the structural grid of the high rise office— building as the canvas upon which to paint his swirling art upon, but that misses the point that both grid and garden were seen as equally important and innovative. For the most part Sullivan slathers the surface of his high rises with ceaseless patterning but here (at CPS) there is a balance that is unique and striking. In terms of Sullivan's ornament development, it is the most perfect of designs or the most perfect of compromises. He has not resolved the contradiction of his art but has decided to celebrate and separate the conflict.

BEEBY AND DESIGN SCHIZOPHRENIA

 I would like to contrast the Sullivan ornament to the more recent experiments in post modern architecture, a neat 100 years from the 1890s to 1990s, by using arguably the best of that period, the Harold Washington Library Center (1992) designed by the firm Hammond Beeby and Babka with the chief designer Thomas Beeby. This is the major statement and structure of the post modern style in Chicago. Here the critique of modernism would be present in one of the most important public buildings. If before the modern style was thought to be cold, impersonal and uncommunicative of its identity and purpose (all glass boxes look alike), then this library would have all the elements that the general public would require and enjoy in understanding its civic importance. No flat roof but an ornamented gabled temple front, no cheap ground floor retail but a battered ashlar granite base, no wimpy aluminum door but a massive stone arch and bronze/glass entry. Go team, Post Modern, GO!

But the schizoid character described in the "Chicago School" buildings still exists in this library building. If you compare the typical plans of the CPS store and the HW library you can see that both have the same even, unaltered square structural grid, plain and simple. And now the exterior in the HW library is even more of a shocking dislocation between the structural bones and the made-up face. The library facade starts with a stone ground floor then on top of it is a masonry wall of five-story arches climaxing in a multistory glass gabled greenhouse roof. The library exterior is one step in a serious of post modern appropriations; the library's tall arched windows are reused from the nearby Auditorium Building by Adler & Sullivan that borrowed the motif from the earlier H. H. Richardson's Marshall Field Warehouse of 1887. This might be the cause of the proportions of the building being a bit chunky and clunky.

The Library's ornament is placed in selected locations; as the carved granite bands at the entry, top/bottom of windows with corn goddess faces and very, very big metal owls and acroteria (flourishes at the gable ends of ancient Greek temples) at the roof top.

For the purpose of brevity I am only discussing one area of ornament on the library: the five, 15-foot tall painted aluminum owls at the cornice. At each of the four corners are barn owls, looking very inscrutable, and over the State Street entry is a larger and very angry horned owl in full wing spread flight, holding a book in its talons.

The owl is a symbol of Minerva, goddess of wisdom in ancient Greek mythology, while the Roman's used the same bird for representing the goddess Athena, also big on wisdom, thus giving it a double vote for knowledge and perspicacity. But there is no precedent for the bird in classical architecture (the Romans did put them on coins). So the owl in the Library is an invented fairy tale character and a tenuous icon for the knowledge of books and libraries. The architect Thomas Beeby art directed the owl's development; the designer Kent Bloomer developed the flame-like acroteria and other ornament behind the birds, while the sculptor Raymond Kaskey designed the figures. Kaskey developed one-third-sized plaster models that were enlarged in Austria, then cast in aluminum at a foundry in Germany, finally shipped to and painted in Chicago.

My confusion on the monumental owl sculptures is that they are a newly invented icon of the Library and not a reference to any element in its history. Their true existence comes from the architect Thomas Beeby's fascination with fairy tales and other myths that might give us an entrance into a richer visual and metaphorical world. He has exhibited several of his charming airbrushed renderings (Magic Marker spray pens?) of fantasy architecture, most notably *The House of Virgil, built in anticipation of the return of the golden age* in the Richard Gray Gallery's *Seven Chicago Architects* show of 1976. That same year that saw the publication of the English version of a book by Bruno Bettelheim, *The Uses of Enchantment: the Meaning*

and Importance of Fairy Tales. The owls here are more the architect's Jungian dream than any logical symbol of the City or its institutions. Therefore the library maintains the Chicago architectural tradition of a split consciousness schizophrenia by simultaneously holding the reality of its logical inner structure with the contradiction of a fantasy mask on its outer facade.

There is one anecdote that I must share which was told to me in my email interview with the talented sculptor of the Library's owls, Raymond Kaskey: at the Library's opening his wife Sherry noted the famous Chicago author Saul Bellow in the crowd and introduced herself and Raymond. Kaskey repeated the silly question that many had asked him that day: was the owl with the open book proceeding to take it out or return it? Bellow noted that in the grand tradition of the Chicago Library, maybe the figure was just stealing it.

Carson Pirie Scott & Co.
(1892 and various additions)
9 E. Madison St.
Architect: Louis Sullivan

Harold Washington
Library Center (1992)
400 S. State St.
Architect:
Hammond Beeby and Babka
Designer: Thomas Beeby
Artist: Kent Bloomer
Owl Artist: Raymond Kaskey

Ornament - Carson Pirie Scott & Co. Building (1892 and various additions) - Architect: Louis Sullivan
Designers: Louis Sullivan and George Grant Elmslie

Right: Harold Washington Library Center Cornice

THE RULES OF CLASSICAL GRAMMAR

GRAHAM ANDERSON PROBST & WHITE
WITH VITRUVIUS

For most of my teenage years I saw these two museums in Chicago as extreme opposite twins: first the Museum of Science and Industry and second the Field Museum of Natural History. Let other children argue about the difference between the Cubs and the White Sox, I knew there was only one local competition that was of any importance and only later in life did it come to my attention that these two institutions were in identical buildings. Well, almost identical, as one has a dome and the other has not.

The Museum of Science and Industry sits in the only original building remaining from the 1893 Chicago Columbian Exposition, but the materials and exhibits from that same Columbian Exposition reside in the other twin, the Field Museum. Then to confuse the chronology, the first museum (Field) started in the location of what was called the Exposition's Fine Arts Building and then later moved 44 blocks uptown to a new building that looked almost exactly like the first building, then the earliest building was rebuilt in the 1930s to be the new/old home of the second museum (Science). What convoluted plot is this?

I could spend hours listing the differences of these two institutions. The "Science" has a full-size submarine and train, while the visiting hyperactive children mostly run between exhibit vitrines pushing the buttons for electronic (now digital) interactive displays and never reading the text (NEVER!). But at the "Field" the studious children would stand in slack-jawed awe at the silent movie-like dioramas, skeletonal dinosaur monsters and cracked crystalline geodes. Class trips with class will win out!

Alas, I know that now the current exhibits are mostly all digital and internetal (made-up word) with no educational differences between these two places. But, I digress.

FIELD MUSEUM OF NATURAL HISTORY

The theme of this essay is to take a large scale public building (museum) in the neoclassical style and compare it to the smallest structure (tomb) made with the same vocabulary by the same architect. The architects for both are Graham Anderson Probst & White, successor firm to the great and powerful Wizard of Oz: D.H. Burnham, with the lead designer being (William) Pierce Anderson. Thereby illustrating how the general concepts of balanced symmetry and the exact definition of specific parts are present, as defined by the ancient Roman writer/engineer Vitruvius within the classical design guidelines for both objects.

There is an accessible and beautifully written tiny book on this very topic by the historian John Summerson titled *The Classical Language of Architecture* (1963) in which he plays with the metaphor of the rules of classical architecture being like Latin lexicon and grammar. In his argument, the five classical columns are icons that

Columbian Exposition's Palace of Fine Arts Building (1893) - Museum of Science and Industry
Architect: Burnham & Root - Designer: Charles Atwood

Side pavilion at the Field Museum of Natural History

are fixed like the immutable rules of Latin's conjugation of verbs and therefore able to make a coherent and understandable design across the centuries.

The Field Museum's classical elements start with a dominating central temple motif "in antis," a term that describes the thick masonry walls that close off the open central colonnade. The immediate adjacent blocks have quotations of a specific structure in the acropolis, the Erechtheion. The farthest wings are colonnades that end with gabled pavilions that duplicate the idea of visually weighting down the ends as seen in the central entry. There are several quotations of the classical lexicon: the Ionic columns are the ones with the curlicue tops, the caryatids are those husky ladies balancing a beam on their heads, the ornament on the roof called the antefix and acroteria being huge leafy flourishes; an entire dictionary of items from the classical vocabulary.

CHALMERS TOMB

If we compare notes on the museum with the Chalmers Tomb (1924), not the most popular gravestone at Graceland Cemetery, we can see that it is not quite a ruin and more of a fragment of a larger imagined building. Perhaps looking a little like the Field Museum's side pavilions without their gable roofs. The tomb is only two fluted Doric columns and two piers with pilasters that hold up a minimal entablature (the collection of the architrave, frieze and cornice in one lintel piece) with the family name inscribed, that is a pretty minimal classical design. The Chalmers Tomb utilizes *The Rules of the (Roman) Road* to establish symmetry, weighted ends, clear quotations from the classical dictionary of column shapes and details. The same rules to make the monster Field Museum building also apply to the minuscule graveyard structure. The tomb is neither a gateway nor a colonnade, not even a temple front, but it is the minimal collection of classical words to make a very short rhetorical sentence: *Vanitatem et Omni Vanitas* (vanity, all is vanity). These are the classical elements that are references which reference only themselves; their function is to recall classical antiquity in a precise romanticism of a long lost and almost forgotten glory.

Note: The architect (William) Pierce Anderson (1870–1924) is also buried at Graceland Cemetery: Edgewood section, lot A, facing north. His own neoclassical family tomb is no match to the Chalmers design and not the most favored by the tourists. The 12-foot tall pink granite assembly is rather like a flat billboard with the four neoclassic Ionic columns framing a wall with the central carved profile of Mr. Anderson. How disappointing that he did not do a fragment of one of his own designs, but then like many architects tombs they are never thought about until it's too late and then designed in default by someone else in the office. I have my own personal gravestone all drawn up, dimensioned and ready to go. I can hardly wait.

William J. Chalmers Tomb (1924) - Graceland Cemetery - 4100 N. Clark St. - Section C, lot 559, space 3
Architect: Graham Anderson Probst & White - Designer: Pierce Anderson

THE MOST PERFECT GEOMETRY

MIES VAN DER ROHE AND LOUIS SULLIVAN

When I first started this essay I discovered that the building I had selected burned down! The Pilgrim Baptist Church caught fire on January 2006 and then on August 2020 a storm collapsed the back brick wall. Scaffolding surrounds the remaining limestone walls. But, because of the determination of its leaders and congregation, there are a number of proposals to restore and update the structure.

The comparison here is between an underrated Miesian modern building, the Carr Memorial Chapel (1952), and a nearby ruin of the 1890s Pilgrim Baptist Church. Both are by famous Chicago architects, who might represent the best of what is called the First Chicago School (1890s) and the later the Post-War Second Chicago School (1950s). Each building exhibits qualities of geometry and order that are pure Architecture. And they are within two blocks of each other.

Louis Sullivan can be reduced to his famous aphorism "Form Ever Follows Function" and Mies van der Rohe to his quotable trademark phrase "Less is More." And yet, I hope that there are more qualities in their work that I can explain in the following pages.

The Pilgrim Baptist Church is perhaps easier to explain: here is a building that exhibits simple geometric forms to establish a sense of order and importance. The four-story base of limestone is like a cube, the roof structure is like a pyramid, the deep entrance arch is like a cylinder. And so the basic geometric forms of the square, triangle and circle are used as the basis of construction. As a religious structure, it was originally a synagogue commission of Dankmar Adler, the engineer and business partner to the designer Louis Sullivan; it has a reason to connect to the elements of the eternal and primary orders of the world. This building was not one of the celebrated works of Sullivan, mostly because it did not have the flourish of vine-like ornament that grew out of his fertile mind.

The second building for comparison is the "God Box" nondenominational Carr Memorial Chapel, designed by Mies. Here we have an extremely simple structure of only masonry bearing walls and steel roof beams. The project exhibits another form of perfect geometry and that is the proportions of the golden rectangle. This is a 5/8 rectangle that when divided into a square magically results in the remaining space to be another golden rectangle and further divisions continue the same. This is mystical mathematical model that architects have used forever. The front elevation dimensions of the Chapel are 23-feet in height and 37-feet in width, with the plan 60-feet in length, do the math and find that it is darn close to the golden rectangle. The interior has a pure simplicity with its centerpiece of a solid travertine altar block that is a miniature of the building's prismatic volume. The proportions of the building and altar are interlocked and reflected in their perfect geometries.

I claim that both buildings show the sacred in their hidden geometries: one of primary solids and the other in proportions of the golden rectangle. Look closely at them both and see the secret hidden wheels and gears of the universe spinning.

Carr Memorial Chapel (1952) - 3360 S. State St. - Architect: Mies van der Rohe

Pilgrim Baptist Church (1891) - 3301 S. Indiana Ave. - Architect: Adler & Sullivan- originally a synagogue

Pilgrim Baptist Church (1891) - 3301 S. Indiana Ave. - Architect: Adler & Sullivan - Burned in fire 2006

Proposal for the Gospel Museum at the Pilgrim Baptist Church - Architect: Dirk Lohan (2008)

Interior - Carr Memorial Chapel

Interior - Pilgrim Baptist Church

NEW MODERN

I hope this book will show you how to walk through the city with open eyes and open heart. This overlooked concrete office building (1959) located at 8704 S. Constance Ave. (87 St.) is banal, beautiful and beguiling.

THE MANMADE MOUNTAIN

JOHN WELLBORN ROOT AND WALTER NETSCH

*Each of these canyons is closed in by a long frontage of towering cliffs and
these soaring walls of brick and limestone and granite rise higher and higher
with each succeeding year, according as the work of erosion at their bases
goes onward—the work of that seething flood of carts, carriages, omnibuses,
cabs, cars, messengers, shoppers, clerks and capitalists, which surges with
increasing violence for every passing day.*

— Henry Blake Fuller (1893), *The Cliff-Dwellers*

Not everyone loved the skyscrapers of Chicago at the turn of the last century.
And yet, now the disparaging quote by the elitist snob of a novelist Henry Blake
Fuller seems like a positive public relations advertisement on the excitement and
adventure in the "Sexy Big City," times have changed.

I have selected two towers, that are surprisingly similar in general size, to
represent the manmade mountain kind of massive built volume that is not a delicate
soaring thing but most definitely appears as a stolid block anchored and unmovable.

The very famous, downtown MONADNOCK BUILDING (1891) was done by
the architectural firm Burnham & Root with the designer John Wellborn Root. It is a
17-story office tower, 70 feet in width, 200 feet in length and 215 feet tall. Its structure
is massive masonry bearing walls that increase in depth as it goes to the ground floor.

The very unloved, near west side, UNIVERSITY HALL (1965) at the University of
Illinois Chicago was done by the large corporate architectural firm of SOM with the
designer and partner in charge as Walter Netsch. This "little skyscraper" is a 28-story
tall building and used for faculty offices, it is 70 feet in width, stepping in length from
150 feet to 170 feet at the top and is 338 feet tall. Its structure is a series of multiplying
concrete columns that increase in number as it goes to the ground floor.

And so these two small high-rise towers that both express their structural support
systems to such an exaggerated degree that they come close to being both irrational
and foolish, therefore most enjoyable. The Monadnock Building is famous as a high
rise structure that limits its cast iron structural elements so that it is almost entirely
made with masonry load-bearing walls some as big as those six-foot thick at its base
and then have that width diminish as it goes higher up the building. This obstinate
belief in masonry only and its simple sculptural articulation of base, cornice and bay
windows has resulted in the building being canonized for holy sainthood in Chicago's
architectural sacred heritage of structural purity.

For the second building I am using the University Hall at the University of
Illinois at Chicago, which is a reinforced concrete frame with six columns, on one
facade, that are widely spaced at the top 14 floors then doubled for the next eight
and subdivided again with more columns for the last five floors. This gives a cluster
of columns near the bottom that is contradicted by a new framing set of six huge
and widely spaced columns with a thick transfer girder for the bottom two floors.
The facade representation is that more loads at the lower levels get carried by more

columns as a cartoon illustration of the structural calculations of support. This is of course absurd as any concrete building just increases the amount of steel reinforcing rods in its standard column outline. My regret is that Netsch did not follow the preposterous logic of the building down to the ground and have a literal forest of different sized and shaped columns populate the entry to the lobby area. Now that would have been something!

Some of Chicago's most famous skyscrapers are explicit and dramatic in their innovative support system: the John Hancock Tower with its monstrous diagonal bracing, McCormick Place and its trussed cantilevered roof, The Daley Center with its long spans plus its 6-foot wide columns and the Willis/Sears Tower with its stepped tubes reinforcing each other in the wind. This Chicago architectural tradition (city of big suspenders) of a tough no-nonsense "build don't talk" kind of town is carried out to the extreme in these two small towers: Monadnock and University Hall. I love both buildings because they are so confident on the outward expression of their existential reality and so utterly oblivious to the faltering truth in that decision, like so many architects that I know.

Cornice at the Monadnock Building (1891) - 53 W. Jackson Blvd.
Architect: Burnham & Root - Designer: John Wellborn Root

Postcard: University Hall (1965) - University of Illinois at Chicago - 1007 W. Harrison St. - Architect: SOM
Designer: Walter Netsch

The Monadnock Building (1891) - 53 W. Jackson Blvd. - Architect: Burnham & Root - Designer: John Wellborn Root

THE COLONNADE, A MOST USEFUL INVENTION

MIES VAN DER ROHE AND OTHERS

The Streeterville neighborhood is a densely packed set of hotels and apartment towers. Walking east, going to the lake on East Chestnut Street, you come to a set of buildings that visually explode out to the wide horizontal elements of expressway, beach and lake. The two apartment towers at 860/880 Lake Shore Drive (1951), by the architect Ludwig Mies van der Rohe, open their ground floors with a continuous colonnade (21-foot column spacing) around both buildings as a supreme gesture that reacts to the site and expansiveness of the lake beyond. It seems obvious now and so many have imitated this effect that it is now a cliché, yet at the moment of its construction it was a revelation.

The colonnade may seem simple and undeniable but it is a piece of Architecture with a capital A. The origin of this invention may be the *stoa* in the Athenian Agora (market square) in ancient Greece, where Socrates, Plato, Aristotle and Zeno taught and discussed philosophy and science; it was a place to stand and view the passing world in all its hundreds of faces. The colonnade is both a dumb shelter from the rain and a profound emblem of the public realm, a focused perspective and a glorification of classical style, it is taken for granted as always existing but is a most wonderful invention. And don't forget the word *stoa* gave its name to the discipline of Stoicism.

Recently Chicago architects have applied the colonnade as part of sun shading or clarifying an entrance. The retail building on Goose Island by Booth Hansen Architects, originally titled Republic Windows (2005), does exactly that with full length shading and columns facing south for the entry. The proportions are slender, delicate and most mechanical in its imagery.

The ION apartment building at 1237 West Fullerton (2007) in the DePaul University campus area, by the architects Antunovich & Assoc., plays with expressing the repeating steel frame of the structure and by pulling the building volume back at the center entry, allowing the engaged frame to evolve to a open colonnade, giving a distinct rhythm to the street.

Finally the climax of two thousand years in the development of western culture is, of course, the McDonald's flagship restaurant (2018) at the Near North Neighborhood on North Clark Street by Ross Barney Architects. With the program to design the fast food joint of the future, the architects have developed various innovations: Internet sales stands, green house gardens, coffee shop lounge floor, diagonal solar panel roof elements and a perimeter colonnade. The McDonald's Flagship, also called the "Rock and Roll McDonald's" after the previous building on this site, is just one of the many modern buildings in Chicago that utilize the invention of the colonnade as both an element of shelter, passive solar energy design and public benefit where in the colonnaded portico at the Agora this ancient phrase was first heard: *scio te ipsum* (know thyself).

Note: The traditional neoclassical colonnades at the Chicago Union Station, Soldier Field and Civic Opera House are not included to allow for a discussion of its more contemporary usage.

860 /880 N. Lake Shore Dr. (1951) - Architect: Mies van der Rohe

Republic Windows and Doors (1998) - 927 W. Evergreen Ave. - Architects: Booth Hansen

ION at Lincoln Park (2007) - 1237 W. Fullerton Ave. - Architect: Antunovich & Assoc.

Chicago McDonald's Flagship Store (2018) - 600 N. Clark St. - Architect: Ross Barney Architects

WHAT IS MONUMENTAL SCALE?

HOLABIRD & ROOT, JACQUES BROWNSON AND CLAES OLDENBURG

Monumental is definitely a term that architects overuse. But, just because something is big does not make it monumental architecture. It has to do with the visual refinements of a pattern of order on the object's surface that communicates a system larger than itself.

In other words: it is monumental if it uses pieces of a monument.

That is a bit of a circular argument and not very helpful, but let me try to explain by specific examples.

JACQUES BROWNSON AND THE DALEY CENTER

One of the best examples of the "monumental" is here in Chicago and illustrates its use in two different styles of buildings. Downtown at the Daley Plaza is the neoclassical Chicago City Hall and County Building (first half built in 1916) and right next door is the rusting modern skyscraper Daley Center (1962).

The City Hall building is monumental because it takes the traditional classical column's three part division of base, shaft and capital and enlarges it enormously. The base is now three-stories, the column is six-stories and the cornice is three-stories tall. It is at a certain level an absurd inflation of a simple architectural element, but that distortion to another dimension of reality is what makes this building monumental. It is an architectural image of the public realm.

The Richard J. Daley Center across the street is a different style but aims for the same effect. This building is more than office spaces; it also has a large number of courtrooms and supporting services. The designer, Jacques Brownson, may be the best of Mies' students for he has taken the vocabulary of the Miesian glass box and raised it to the next level of scale. The columns are 6 feet, 4 inches in width and they span the enormous distance of 87-feet. The building is so big that it belongs to a separate set of structures, something more like a pier for a bridge than for an office space. To continue the bridge metaphor, all floors in the Daley Center are made of an unbelievable seven-foot tall steel truss that, in reality, could come from a bridge design.

So you can see two types of Monumental buildings right next to each other for visual comparison. The City Hall takes the vocabulary of neoclassical architecture and enlarges it to an American scale of bigness and the Daley Center takes the vocabulary of modern architecture and enlarges it to a super steroid, muscle man size, the result is a definition of the public realm that is vast and intentionally intimidating.

CLAES OLDENBURG AND THE CHICAGO FIREPLUG

There is one variant of the definition of the monumental, in that, instead of an enormous size it is an object that has an undetermined size. A confusion and ambiguity of what are we looking at and how big it is. Usually, that means no visible clues like people-sized doors or windows and manageable steps on stairs.

Postcard: Chicago City Hall (1911) -121 N. LaSalle St. - Architect: Holabird & Root
North side of the same building is the County Building

Richard J. Daley Center (1965) - 50 W. Washington St. - Architect: C. F. Murphy Assoc.
Designer: Jacques Brownson - originally the Chicago Civic Center

In other words: it is monumental if you can't figure out how big it really is.

The manipulations of the artist Claes Oldenburg on the presence of the patented Chicago Fireplug or the Chicago Fire Hydrant or the CWW 1916 (Chicago Water Works) or the Double 4 ½ inch Hydrant allow an almost nondescript functional piece of the streetscape, previously all but invisible, to become an iconic element of the city.

The artist has projected a monumental scale on a typical nondescript object, illustrating the interchangeable effects of the miniature and the monumental. This may seem contradictory but the utilitarian fire hydrant is in its abstract geometric shape, its strange anthropomorphic outline and its alien-like mechanical operation (opened by the biggest wrench possible) making it something that can be imagined as something else, or more distinctly, as something else but enormous.

Monumental scale can be most simply defined as a "magical illusion" in which the large and the very small can be interchanged by the manipulation of the artist or architect. So, like the poem, the expansiveness of the universe can be found in William Blake's grain of sand.

In his long career, Oldenburg has produced a marvelous series of sculptures that enlarge everyday objects to monumental size, and in my opinion, act as both a comment on crude popular culture, satirized art history and rude sexual symbols. You can always find gigantic genitalia hiding in his work and the Chicago fireplug series is no exception. In the inverted fireplug pieces Oldenburg has stated his mimicking of the high artist, Brancusi in his *Torso of a Young Man* which in itself is mimicking an erect penis.

In 1968, Oldenburg was knocked around by the cops during the Democratic Party Convention police riots in the city. That year Oldenburg took the Chicago fireplug and proposed it as a skyscraper in several different locations and conditions. I believe it is certainly meant to be an insult to the existing political order at the time. To be direct, I am stating the humble fireplug can be seen in the artist's work as a metaphoric shape of female form in its two breasts of the extended pipes and hex-bolt nipples and when inverted as a metaphor of the male form that re-imagines the supply base as a penis and the two circular cover plates as testicles. It is all a very neat trick of ambiguous visualization to make a point on the absurdity of the skyscraper as a serious piece of art and the corrupt culture behind its construction.

Or is it just about the joy of seeing everything in the world as an animated quality that speaks to the child in each of us and the devil in each child?

Note: Claes Oldenburg produced a 101-foot tall public sculpture titled *Batcolumn* at 600 West Madison Avenue in 1977.

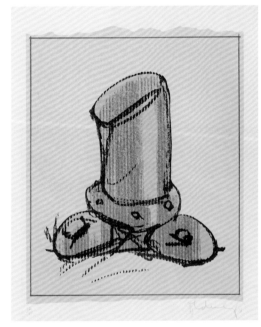

Claes Oldenburg
Soft Fire Plug, Inverted, 1973
(printed 1972; signed 1973)
color lithograph
on Hodgkinson
handmade paper
40 x 30 3/4 in.
(101.6 x 78.1 cm)
© Claes Oldenburg

Claes Oldenburg, *Proposed Colossal Monument for End of Navy Pier, Chicago: Fireplug (Two Views), 1968*, pencil on paper
30 x 22 in. (76.2 x 55.88 cm), © Claes Oldenburg

GLASS BOXES AND METAL CUBES

SOM AND JOHN RONAN

In our time when most new Chicago office buildings are monstrously out of scale, big cancerous lumps of poisonous real estate (not mentioning any names because you know who you are, new skyscraper buildings on the Chicago River) it is quite a shock to see modern, rectangular steel and glass buildings of a manageable scale and sensuous materials. I offer these two structures as a hopeful example that not all members of their style and ilk are evil and destructive.

INLAND STEEL

The Inland Steel Building (1957) by the architects SOM with the designer Walter Netsch (and arguably others) is only 17 floors in height so it is most certainly a volume that is easily visually digestible to a citizen on the sidewalk. The materials are not the usual black painted steel of the era but glitzy polished stainless steel with a brilliant color matching of natural green tinted glass. The facade could be considered an advertisement for use of the material of the owners company: Inland Steel. The building's glass box shape is modulated by vertically articulated exterior columns and a completely separate 25-story service tower of elevators, stairs and washrooms at the east side, so the glass box seems broken down into smaller pieces to be an even more accessible size.

The lobby at the south end is completely visible through its large glass panel storefront with the original wire sculpture (continuing the theme of stainless steel) by the artist Richard Lippold, titled *Radiant 1,* sitting in a shallow pool. Most wonderful is the recent addition by the architect Frank Gehry of a security desk made from large chunks of stacked slag green glass, appearing as if a bright green plastic "transformer" monster toy has captured the security guard.

Out of all the miles and miles of esoteric curtain wall details that contemporary architects obsess with this building jumps over those technical refinements to the bigger picture and maybe accidentally makes something profoundly beautiful.

POETRY FOUNDATION

The second building to be examined is the Poetry Foundation (2011), located in the River North neighborhood, and designed by John Ronan Architects and a mere two (tall) stories in height but a wonderful example of the modern metal and glass aesthetic. This houses the officers of *Poetry Magazine* (founded in 1912) and contains a public non-circulating library, gallery and theater. The glass box of the building proper is wrapped by a freestanding steel frame with a metal screen and opened at the north east corner to establish the entry and a small garden space (give the trees some years to grow).

The obscuring zinc metal screens, the relentlessly repeated building vertical module and the eroded corner opening create a scale-less monumentality for

Inland Steel Building (1956)
30 Monroe St. - Architect: SOM
Designer: Walter Netsch and others

Poetry Foundation (2011) - 61 W. Superior St. - Architect: John Ronan Architects

the little building by obscuring the real size of the entry door, any relatable sized windows or openings. This gives the building a greater scale and presence than would be normal for a two-story structure but it also fails to give any symbolic development to connect to the Poetry Foundation's public functions and the unfortunate result is that its abstract form and materials can be found in many high design parking garages (sorry, I don't have a Chicago example). Perhaps the typical modern solution to note the cultural importance of any modern glass box building is to plop a big pretentious abstract sculpture in the foreground. With this building we are left with only a tasteful Helvetica graphic statement at the sidewalk for satisfying that need. The opportunity for a commissioned Chicago artist to weave a poetic visual statement in the pattern of the metal screens is still not lost (hint, hint).

These two examples show sensitivity to scale, texture and color lost in most tall modern buildings and hopefully serve as inspiration for others to follow and perhaps demand.

Inland Steel Building (1956) - Artist: Richard Lippold: lobby *Radiant 1* - Artist: Frank Gehry: glass lobby desk (2018)

MANNERISM OR MISTAKES?

NETSCH VS MIES AND GARDEN VS SULLIVAN

Mannerism is an art historical term invented to describe the art and architecture produced immediately after the Italian Renaissance. Not quite the later florid Baroque and certainly not like its precursor, the rule defined Renaissance, but something in-between.

In the architecture profession this term has been used indiscriminately to describe any weirdo distortion or conscious misapplication of the rules of an existing style or architectural system, like the defined orders of classical columns. Then there is the basic question when confronted with this attitude: is it possible that the mannerist architect had just made dumb mistakes and not tried to create a stylistic revolution?

At one time Chicago architects were very rigid and doctrinaire, so it is pretty easy to spot their opposites in the iconoclastic distortions of the big Chicago style gods.

WALTER NETSCH VERSUS MIES VAN DER ROHE

The story of Mies reluctantly escaping Nazi Germany in 1938 to a job teaching at the Armour Institute (later Illinois Institute of Technology) has been discussed elsewhere. But the job offer also included the extra bonus of being the college's architect and 20 years of in-house commissions.

But all good things must come to a bitter end, when in 1952 the president of IIT moved over to the same position at NYU, the new administration looked at the meticulous and slow, very slow architect in charge, they decided to move onto other options and chose a big corporate firm, Skidmore Owings and Merrill (SOM), to do their next new structures. Boy, was Mies pissed! And that is why you find Mies' personal library, of 600 volumes, donated to the University of Illinois at Chicago and not IIT.

And so the rigid formula designed by Mies for the buildings at IIT—an orthogonal module that controls and dictates all design decisions from large scale site planning to small scale placement of bathroom floor tiles was now ripe for change, adaptation or just plain screwing it up.

The designer Walter Netsch at SOM was the first architect to operate on the IIT campus without the Mies seal of approval or overview. His design of the Paul V. Galvin Library (originally the Crerar Library) is, for my purposes, a perfect example of mannerism in contemporary architecture, because the style that is being manipulated, is not classical Rome, but the post-war Midwest modernism.

The exemplar that I am using for comparison is not the unbuilt Mies design for the same library but his design for Crown Hall, a masterpiece of a vast open volume drafting hall (drafty hall?) for the Institute's Architecture Department. The strategy of Netsch was to follow, in general, the visual image of Mies' Crown Hall but not follow in the specifics. So we have a set of simple opposites in the design of the new building.

Crown Hall is associated with the tradition of German neoclassical buildings by having a carefully proportioned set of travertine steps and platforms that lead to a symmetric entry at the *piano nobile* (raised main floor). Then in the Netsch building you had to go the opposite way—down not up to a utilitarian modern set of glass entry doors. Confusion coming from turning the rules upside down (up is down and down is up) is a prime characteristic of historic mannerist architecture.

Crown Hall had meticulously detailed columns supporting its steel roof girders (7-feet height and 120-feet length). In contrast, the Netsch building has the columns recessed and hidden inside the building facade so the huge steel girders seem to be resting on the roof without visible support. Confusion of support and weightlessness is a prime characteristic of historic mannerist architecture.

Also the Netsch building fails to understand the Miesian site plan of the campus. Originally, Mies had two major buildings, the Library/Administration and the Student Union, placed symmetrically opposite each other on Thirty-Third Street and making a central public space between them. The Netsch buildings, Galvin Library and Hermann Hall, are similar in location, size, materials and roof girders, but fail miserably in making the space between them anything but two disconnected grass lawns. The unbuilt Mies buildings would have succeeded because he had carefully organized a set of separate entrances on both buildings that faced each other and which would have activated the space, while giving meaningful enclosing walls to this little, unsuccessful Chicago piazza. This would have been a world of difference from the black blank walls that Netsch had built.

There are other more subtle details to argue about in comparisons (the library's concrete panel base), but in the Galvin Library Netsch struggled with confronting the master on his own turf (remember the grass lawns) and being torn from being either innovative and discordant or sympathetic and submissive. This is a perfectly fine psychological conflict for defining a kind of "mannerism."

On the other hand, perhaps I give too much credit to Netsch for an intricate manipulation of an existing Miesian system, maybe the Galvin Library is not as mannerist as I believe but just a series of "mistakes."

The last note on the Galvin Library building is that it received the ultimate insult by not being listed in the encyclopedic *AIA Guide to Chicago*. Because it just wasn't pretty enough.

HUGH GARDEN VERSUS LOUIS SULLIVAN

I was first introduced to the wonderful world of quirky Chicago architecture by the architect/author Stuart Cohen in his 1976 book *Chicago Architects*. That book was to enlighten the world that Chicago architects were more than producers of structural grid wallpaper and in reality a plurality of attitudes and styles were of equal importance in the city.

The Chapin and Gore Building of 1904 was described in that volume as an example of mannerist qualities that used the noble "First Chicago School" as the straight man for the basis of its jokes in architect Hugh Garden's facade design.

The Chapin and Gore Building starts at the top with its upmost 5 floors using the very standard Chicago brick piers reflecting the spacing of the structural columns beyond, with the infill of the "Chicago Window" pattern. This window has one central fixed glass pane flanked by two double hung windows for ventilation, but the lower you go down the facade, you'll find that all hell breaks loose.

Crown Hall (1956) - 3360 S. State St.- Architect: Mies van der Rohe

Galvin Library (1962) - 35 W. 33rd. St. - Architect: SOM - Designer: Walter Netsch

Chapin and Gore Building (1904) - 63 Adams St. - Architect: Schmitt & Garden - Designer: Hugh Garden

Chapin and Gore Building (1904) - 63 Adams St. - Architect: Schmitt & Garden - Designer: Hugh Garden

Floors two and three (originally the storage area for the booze company Chapin and Gore) develop peculiar window groupings that establish an ornament surrounding band and then breaks it, remember mannerism's mischief. Further, this same unusual window design pulls both floors into an image of one *piano nobile* level, while prominently placed lion's head gargoyles (crazy?) poke out from the flat masonry wall. Curiouser and curiouser, as Alice in Wonderland would say.

I would have to acknowledge that the very unmodern lion head gargoyles also appear on the second floor of Louis Sullivan's Bayard building (1898) in New York City. Maybe this is a "mannerist" quotation?

But the final magic trick on the facade is on the ground floor where the brick piers above disappear and a pair of symmetric entries makes a void, an empty recess for the doors, giving its own image of instability. H. Allen Brooks has written on this in his book *The Prairie School, Frank Lloyd Wright and his Midwest Contemporaries* as a point of "mannerist tension."

The Chapin and Gore Building lost its cornice and column capitals in the 1950s but it still has a great deal of power in that the designer, Hugh Garden, has been able to dazzle us with his prestidigitation that has been ignored for so many years.

SULLIVAN AT THE GAGE BUILDING

As a quick aside, walk east on Adams Street from Chapin and Gore to Michigan Avenue and then two blocks north to the three buildings collectively called the Gage Buildings (18, 24 and 30 South Michigan Avenue). The first two buildings by Holabird & Roche (1899) would be called generic "Chicago School," but the northernmost structure has a special facade design by Louis Sullivan. It is not uncommon, even today, for big name designers to do only the facade of a predesigned building, so as to juice-up an uninteresting building's appearance.

This facade is a new and cheaper reality that Sullivan had to face in his latter career, after his partner Adler left him during the economic panic of 1893. It forced him to concentrate his ornamental flourishes in a limited area for maximum visual impact. For this building what do we call the ornament at the top of the two central columns, too big for a column capital, too small for a cornice? Would the plant metaphor of a rose blooming on top of its stem be too romantic?

So we are using all three of the Gage Buildings to contrast with the later Chapin and Gore structure. The first two Gage's are the simplest version of the "Chicago School" tall buildings that Chapin and Gore reacted to, distorted and embellished in a mannerist manner. The last Gage from Sullivan's pen might be called the first step in the last phase of his career. Simpler and smaller buildings in a series of one-story banks, that are forced to make a composition of large blank areas with isolated ornamented explosions.

Rejoice in the fireworks display in front of you.

Ornament at Gage Building (1899) - Facade Designer: Louis Sullivan

Chicago, Ill.   The Millinery Bldg on Michigan Ave

Postcard: Gage Building (1899)
18 S. Michigan Ave. Architect:
Holabird & Roche Facade
Designer: Louis Sullivan

POST MODERN

Royal Pawn Shop located at 428 S. Clark St. The Russian Constructivist dream of architecture as a pure electric propaganda machine is illustrated here.

SIGNS AND SYMBOLS

MAGIKIST, RAPP & RAPP AND LOUIS SULLIVAN

Once upon a time in the land of Chicago there were three monstrous elevated flashing neon signs of the silhouette of kissing red lips advertising the carpet cleaning company MAGIKIST (short for the magical kiss trademark). Since the company went under in 2001 the signs have all been removed, but that surrealist graphic design always represented to me something wonderful about Chicago: its blue collar uniqueness, its coarse commercialness and its uninhibited wackiness. Maybe that's all gone now, as the entire design world slips into corporate sameness, but I miss it.

The idea that Chicago has merged the huge commercial sign and the supporting building deserves a special unique word: Magikistness. You heard it here first.

THE CHICAGO THEATER SIGN

The 74-foot tall vertical building sign that is called "the Ambassador of the City of Chicago" is the one attached to the landmark Chicago Theater (1921) on North State Street by Rapp & Rapp Architects. I will admit I have never been inside the building as my snobbish thespian taste leans more to the smaller avant-garde theater groups that populate Chicago's cultural scene. The building has been described in official statements as "neo-baroque french-revival style" and I will admit that I have no idea what that means. But the vertical marquee sign in its lurid neon font, over-publicized and over-the-top excess is quite wonderful. Perhaps it is equal to the 25-foot tall electronic advertising sign "Welcome to Fabulous Las Vegas" stuck in the traffic median strip of Las Vegas Boulevard or the 50-foot tall alien invasion HOLLYWOOD letters in the hills of Griffin Park, Los Angeles. All three have in common a surrealist dislocation of reality and flash card familiarity. They are both monumental and empty of content, containing words that have been forgotten even as you read them.

KRAUSS MUSIC STORE

I want to juxtapose that Chicago Theater sign as an emblem of the downtown tourist city with a small and almost forgotten Louis Sullivan building in the Lincoln Park neighborhood: the Krauss Music Store (1922). Perhaps the last work by the architect, who died in 1924. The central ornamental vertical sign inflates the importance of this tiny two-story building by making a heraldic object with a certain ambiguity: is it an advertising sign, a flagpole, an enlarged key or a jewelry stick pin? Since the music company is long gone, the central letter "K" in the parapet makes the ornamental figure even more ambiguous (Das Kapital!). Of all Sullivan's late works this becomes a unique hybrid object of sign and building.

LASALLE TOWERS APARTMENTS

The last sign/building merger that I wish to examine is the LaSalle Towers Apartments (1981) at North LaSalle Street by the architects Weese Seegers Hickey Weese and Murals by artist Richard Haas. The original building (1922) was a pretty dumpy high rise brick box hotel with little to commend it. The architects with great ingenuity and charm transformed the gutted 19-story block with a new window treatment and a commission to the artist Richard Haas to paint full-size murals onto the tower. The art works are titled *Homage to the Chicago School of Architecture*. For the south side he appropriates the decorative surround on the oculus at the Louis Sullivan's Merchants National Bank in Grinnell, Iowa (1914) and then at the bottom he abstracts the typical monumental arch that Sullivan placed on his 1893 Transportation Building with historic figures at the base. The murals are a way

The Magikist sign towering over an expressway (circa 2000)
Removed 2001

to upscale the limitations of the renovated block and they also are successful in the meta-narrative of the identity of the architecture. The use of painted recall of historic ornament here is acceptable in a modernist dogma because it is isolated in quotation marks. It is more of a sign of ornament, a subtle signifier of a desire not consummated. The vertical assembly of fake windows climaxing in the Sullivan oculus window is a sign in two ways, literally and expressively of ornament as a Freudian hidden desire.

Note: In 2020 the adjacent lot to the LaSalle Towers Apartments was developed and the lower three floors of the south Haas mural were covered up and destroyed.

The Chicago Theater Sign (1921)
175 N. State St.
Architect: Rapp & Rapp

Krauss Music Store (1922)
4611 N. Lincoln Ave.
Architect: Louis Sullivan

Painted mural at the LaSalle Towers Apartments (1981) -1211 N. LaSalle St.
Architect: Weese Seegers Hickey Weese - Artist: Richard Haas

THE HIDDEN FACE IN THE FACADE

ANGELS, GARGOYLES , KEYSTONES, CARYATIDES, BRACKETS, BUFFALOES AND FULL FACE FACADES

It is one of the great pleasures of strolling along the sidewalks of Chicago (North Side, South Side, all around the town) is catching a glimpse of a stone face watching you pass by. Here are just a few of my favorites, I hope you make a list of your own.

ANGELS AND OCULI—224 S. MICHIGAN AVENUE

Yes, I know every church has a squadron of angels on its facade or interior murals. What I am searching for is the placement of these ethereal beings where they do not belong, at the site of the profane and not the sacred. That is why I adore the angels and oculi (circular windows) in the top floor of the old Sante Fe Building now called 224 South Michigan Avenue by Burnham & Co. (1904). They are really hard to see and may require binoculars but they are worth it (serious angel spotting). What is going on exactly? The very vertical postured female angels flanked by palm branches, spiral wreaths at their feet and interspaced with a pure circular window and its upside-down keystone; it does not seem to be any type of standard Beaux-Arts composition. We are all amateur archaeologists looking at the hieroglyphics of an ancient tribe of architects called the "First Chicago School," who lived over a century ago. I am at a loss to explain and can only request you to enjoy.

GARGOYLES—COBB GATE

We all know that the University of Chicago is where Harry Potter really wanted to go to college but couldn't pass the admissions test. The historic campus has a plethora of stone carved gargoyles, mythic creatures from medieval times, covering its neo-gothic structures. So listing the Cobb Gate as my first choice for gargoyles is pretty arbitrary. But more than their ugly faces and low level for better viewing, it is the legend of the gate, which students pass down from graduate to undergraduate that attracts me. For on this structure the stone grotesques dot the triangle of the gate's facade in a step by step assembly, which connects to the school legend in that the bottom row of creatures represent the horrid and evil admission proctors, then the next row up are the freshmen, then the next line the sophomores, next the juniors and the last monster standing at the apex is the triumphant senior. In my mind the last is the ultimate heartless monster, the right-wing, free-market economics major that the University is so famous for. With that in mind, the Latin inscription over the entry should read: *Custulam, Eruntque Comedentes* (let them eat cake).

KEYSTONES—THALIA BUILDING

The nice thing about Chicagoans is that they are so generous in tearing down their historic buildings and then selling the broken ornament scrap to appease the world's museums. That is why you find the best Sullivan elevator door in Los Angeles and the best Chicago stone keystone face in the Brooklyn Museum. That particular keystone came from 2222 South Wabash Avenue, a demolished building with a dark history and once the site of an infamous gambling den called The Four Deuces, and of course Al Capone lived next door. The face is spectacular with its hellacious leonine visage, leafy beard and surround, best of all it fits into a very specific type of keystone face: "The Green Man." This medieval myth was described in a 1939 article on carved ornamental faces in historic British churches, from then on it grew into a jungle of weirdness. The NYU scholar Carolyn Dinshaw wrote a charming essay in the book *The Middle Ages in the Modern World* on how the myth was appropriated by a U.S. gay rights group The Radical Faeries in 1979 in the continued evolution of a powerful allegory on nature versus culture.

But Chicago has more "Green Men" keystone faces with the best being in the Near South Side neighborhood of Pilson on the main entry arch of The Thalia, a historic theater building and now multiple bars. The face is easy to spot with its oak leaf beard, thistle hair and most cheerful mug; it seems to project its job description as mellow beer-filled welcomer, certainly not the radical ecological destroyer of the industrial poisoned world of man.

CARYATIDES—FIELD MUSEUM OF NATURAL HISTORY

Caryatides are female figured sculptures of slaves, condemned to carry, on their heads, the crushing weight of their conscience and guilt forever and ever. They are derived from a single source in ancient Greece: the smallish building on the Acropolis titled the Erechtheion.

As I have explained before, the Museum of Science and Industry and the Field Museum of Natural History are siblings that have much of the same design, both coming from the 1893 Columbian Exposition. Both have sets of multiple caryatides on their entry facades. I doubt that most visitors to the museums even notice these objects. With their faces emotionless and their arms unexpressive, I just have given up on engaging them any more than a brief glance and hello.

BRACKETS—APARTMENT BUILDING IN LINCOLN PARK

At the north-east corner of the intersection of West Arlington Place and North Orchard Street in the neighborhood of Lincoln Park is a five-story yellow brick apartment building (1915) that can only be described as arts and crafts/Egyptoid. I am most interested in the cast concrete brackets at the three entry canopies. They are a wonderful collision of a single triglyph, a single guttae, swirls, spirals with other bits and bobs, to make a most peculiar hidden face in the facade. The talking door knob from *Alice in Wonderland* (the Disney movie) came to mind and other fever dreams. What is most marvelous is how the face appears and then disappears in your perception, a trick of figure/ground readings that are constantly shifting.

BUFFALOES—CHICAGO BOARD OF TRADE

When as a small child I first saw the carved stone buffalo heads (artist Alvin Meyer) at the north entry of the Chicago Board of Trade Building and I thought how logical that they gave this animal a feathered headdress of an American Indian Chief (a tribal figure holding corn stalks is nearby at the central entry clock), because after all, what could be more American than making building ornament from the culture of the plains tribesman? No, that's not correct. The ornament is some ancient Sumerian or Babylonian decorative motif, because those were the first guys to plant wheat. I still think my misreading was more relevant and poetic, but then most misreadings are.

This buffalo face on the facade is a wonderful stylized creature: part art deco gem, part dark nightmare, part stupid cow. In a similar way the ancient Greeks decorated the frieze of some of their temples with the image of a bull's skull called Bukrania. For the Greeks, it was about spiritual sacrifice to the gods, but for the Chicagoans it is about trading future market shares, our own gods.

FULL FACE FACADE—JACK-O-LANTERN BUILDING

This four-story stone structure at 149 West Chicago Avenue (1891) is most certainly qualified for the award of the most unrecognized and unloved building in this essay. In fact I don't know if it will survive until the publication of this book. To me the jack-o-lantern face is quite obvious. The elements of the face start with the braced arch on the second floor as most definitely a mouth with two front teeth, the symmetric arched window at the third floor are the eyes with the small rectangular widow in the center as the nose. When we go to the top floor I see the widows as eyebrows and the top most date/plaque/parapet as a unique Chicago pompadour hair style. As with most carved pumpkins for Halloween the cut-out expressions are both amusing and one full of pain.

FULL FACE FACADE—ANTI-CRUELTY SOCIETY

The architect Stanley Tigerman produced a facade of puzzle pieces in his 1979 addition to the 1930s two-story limestone box of the original Anti-Cruelty Society. The pattern of those windows is where a dog's face is presented in the theme of *How Much is That Doggie in the Window* used in animal adoption. The architect has his trademark re-entry curve making a window in the shape of basset hound's floppy ears, then the central arched opening is to be the mouth/nose and the top of the head is the cut-out arch in the front parapet.

The post modern era was for some architects an excuse for giddy excess of wild forms and colors, but for others it was a serious way to communicate the essence of the building beyond the limited vocabulary of modernism. For this animal shelter the humorous face is a mask hiding the tragic truth that most of its residents will not be adopted and will be eventually euthanized.

FULL FACE FACADE—GAGE BUILDING

The last of the three buildings on Michigan Avenue called the Gage Buildings had its facade designed by the architect Louis Sullivan in 1899. I have talked about Sullivan's indiscriminate plastering of his floral ornament on all surfaces and materials of some of his buildings, but here, for economics or aesthetics the ornament is limited and carefully placed. The efflorescence at the top of the two central columns are decorative things that are hard to classify; advertisement or column capital or frieze ornament? They are for me the most sublime faces done on any Chicago building. At one moment they are a fairy tale god and the next a cloud of the north wind, a visage in smoke or a leafy green monster. For years and years, they have look eastwardly across the lake and I wonder, what have they seen and what storm is coming?

ANGELS AND OCULI - Santa Fe Centre (1904) - 224 S. Michigan Ave.- Architect: Burnham & Co.

GARGOYLES
Cobb Gate (1893)
University of Chicago
E. 57 St. at Ellis Ave.
Architect: Henry Ives Cobb

KEYSTONES
The Four Deuces
2222 South Wabash Ave.
now at The Brooklyn Museum

KEYSTONES
Thalia Hall (1893)
1807 Allport St.
Architect:
Faber & Pagels

BRACKETS - Apartment building (1915)
NE corner of W. Arlington Pl. and
N. Orchard St. - Architect: Unknown.

CARYATIDES - Field Museum of Natural History (1920)
Architect: Graham Anderson Probst & White - Artist: Henry Hering

BUFFALOES -Chicago Board of Trade (1930) - 141 W. Jackson Blvd.
Architect: Holabird & Root - Artist: Alvin Meyer

FULL FACE FACADE - Jack-O-Lantern Building (1891) - 149 W. Chicago Ave.
Architect: Unknown

FULL FACE FACADE - Anti-Cruelty Society (1979) - 510 N. LaSalle Dr.
Architect: Stanley Tigerman & Assoc.– renovated in 2011

FULL FACE FACADE - Gage Building (1899) -18 S. Michigan Ave
Architect: Holabird & Roche - Facade Designer: Louis Sullivan

BRICKS AND THEIR LOVE OF ARCHES

LOUIS KAHN, STANLEY TIGERMAN AND FUGARD & KNAPP

The great American architect, Louis I. Kahn, had his own patented, signature statements to match Sullivan and Mies. One of his much quoted lines is: "You say to a brick, 'What do you want, brick?' And the brick says to you 'I like an arch.'" That statement could be considered an aphorism or jingoism, a fairy tale or a *fait accompli*, it is both Talmudic and mystical. Kahn never did a building in Chicago, but like most strong architectural images they filter down through other architects in unexpected ways: by inspiration or appropriation.

PIPER'S ALLEY PARKING GARAGE

The infamous Chicago architect Stanley Tigerman (who died in 2019) had a series of buildings being built in Bangladesh in the 1970s at the same time as Kahn was completing the National Assembly Building in Dhaka (started 1961 and completed in 1982) with other structures. Tigerman was well acquainted with Kahn's work through firsthand experience. The austere geometric style of Kahn's brick arches (or cutouts in a brick wall) was lifted in a five-fingered discount by Tigerman for a much more downscale set of projects on Chicago's eastern end of North Avenue: a one-story retail building and a five-story parking garage (1977). Their facades are an assembly of circular arches, round arches, flat arches, round arches with under arches, collisions of arches and broken arches. The garage is the most dramatic with its even repetition of arches that are visibly out of synch with the concrete structural columns immediately behind. The flatness and thinness of the brick wall negates any reading of the masonry as supporting or structural. And so we have a red-brown masonry scrim of a purely theatrical nature. The sacred mystical work of Kahn is transformed to the rather profane entry of a Walgreens drug store. And yet...

Are these two buildings (the garage and the Walgreens) standing as pre-post modern architecture or maybe just a bad vaudeville joke? Or are they are the best illustration in Chicago of architecture-as-language and its possible semantic manipulation? Is this our own little example of the idea of mannerism? That rather unloved style that came after the austere Renaissance, when all bets were off and anything goes. Or as King Richard has noted: "Now is the winter of our discontent" and the anarchist desire for change and escape from the boredom of a limited bourgeoisie culture. Here is an example of Chicago's architectural profession fighting with its own identity and definition in the world. These two funny little buildings are worth looking at and understanding.

THE MOODY CHURCH

For a contrast on these weighty masonry themes, just a short walk of two blocks east is The Moody Church of 1925 by the architects Fugard & Knapp. Named after its first pastor in the nineteenth century, Dwight Lyman Moody, and part of the boom construction in neighborhood churches in the 1920s throughout the city. It is being used here as a foil to the thin scrim of masonry on the Tigerman buildings to show the elaborate refined detailing of brick as a complicated ornament that both holds up the edifice and delights in showing off in all its multitude of construction possibilities.

The building is mostly a steel structure at the auditorium with the elaborate masonry detailing and ornament of a period that might be derived from German brick gothic of the 1500s. The publicity statements of the church noting its building's connection to the design of the ancient Roman structure (turned into mosque) of St. Sophia in Istanbul, Turkey is way off the mark. But the sheer exuberance of the masonry work is the reason it is included in this chapter. Almost every type of masonry manipulation is present: aedicules, belt courses, brackets, batters (opposite of a corbel), buttresses, columns, modified common bonding pattern (I don't know what this strange pattern is really called), corbels, cornice arcades, dentils, various diaper bonding patterns (zigzag diagonals), dog's-tooth corners, flat arches (jack arches), jamb blocks, keystones, lintels, oculi (bull's-eye arches), pilasters, piers, pointed segmented arches (inside), projecting headers and projecting rowlocks (sometimes together), round arches, round arches with alternating projecting brick voussoirs, running bonding pattern, et cetera and et cetera. All within the non-structural masonry walls enclosing the building's steel frame. Enjoy the explosion of delight in front of you!

If The Moody Church does its ornament in four courses of brick and the Piper Alley Parking Garage does it in two courses of brick, there is one building that does it in one course or thinner. And here I am interjecting a building not in Chicago and not even alive today, but still one of the great fantasy structures of modern architecture: the *grosse schauspielhaus* of 1919 in Berlin by the architect Hans Poelzig.

GROSSE SCHAUSPIELHAUS (LARGE PLAYHOUSE)

A huge single-story theater for the dramatic arts that had some of the first spectaculars by the famous avant-garde director Max Reinhardt, think hundreds of actors on the stage chanting in unison, that was renovated by Poelzig with the thinnest possible arcaded forms illuminated with colored lights, think stalactites and rainbows. The entire assembly is considered one of the great "expressionist" works of architecture, something that Chicago is lacking a single example. So I am forcing a leap of imagination on the reader to visualize the 1925 (land purchased in 1917) arcaded and vaulted Moody Church interior of 4,000 seats merging in their mind's-eye with the 1919 arcaded and vaulted *grosse schauspielhaus* of 3,400 seats (no balcony). Irrespective of the solemnity of a church and the show-biz dazzle of a theater this is a thought experiment in comparing two very similar interior volumes and seeing how close and how far Chicago's artistic design has been and still is.

Ayub Central Hospital (1975) - Dhaka,
Bangladesh - Architect: Louis Kahn
(now Shaheed Suhrawardy
Medical College & Hospital)

Piper's Alley Mall and Parking
(1977) - 230 W. North Ave.
Architect: Stanley Tigerman

Postcard: The Moody Church (1925) - Architect: Fugard & Knapp

Piper's Alley Mall and Parking (1977) - 230 W. North Ave. - Architect: Stanley Tigerman

Detail - The Moody Church (1925)
North Ave. and Clark St.
Architect: Fugard and Knapp

Detail - Walgreens Store
(1977) - 1601 N. Wells St.
Architect: Stanley Tigerman

Postcard: The Moody Church (1925) - North Ave. and Clark St. - Architect: Fugard and Knapp

Grosse Schauspielhaus (1919) - Berlin, Germany - Architect: Hans Poelzig

THE VAULT AND THE SKY

PHILIP JOHNSON, THOMAS BEEBY AND FRANK GEHRY

The post modern style was highly successful in designing interiors, whether it was the acceptance of ornament, color, texture or historic styles many rooms of that period resonated with memorable qualities. The rooms chosen here move in a logical progression and each operates in a way that tries to open the ceiling to a metaphor of the sky. The Philip Johnson lobby has a historic plaster vaulted ceiling covered in gold leaf, the Thomas Beeby room has a greenhouse glass vaulted ceiling and the Frank Gehry exterior music pavilion has a interlocking metal trellis for both mounting speakers and enclosing the space around the audience lawn. The Architect-Speak phrase might be "dematerialization" to describe the opening up of the ceiling from plaster, to glass, to trellis and finally to sky.

GOLD LEAF VAULTED CEILING
190 SOUTH LASALLE STREET (1986)

Philip Johnson was more than an architect, he was a theatrical impresario whose biography (good and bad) is too long and complicated to discuss here. But the only building he did in Chicago is quite an explosion of post modern ideas. The facade of 190 South LaSalle Street is an abstraction and appropriation of a long demolished Chicago Landmark the Masonic Temple of 1892. And like most of Johnson's post modern towers various influences and styles are integrated or crushed together in one glorious mess. The lobby has nothing to do with the theme of the facade but that doesn't bother me. Johnson has been allowed to wow the audience with using the entire ground floor for a theatrical stage set of a lobby. With its 55-foot tall ceilings, tomato soup colored marble walls, patterned black and white marble floors, serious Corinthian column capitals and the hangman stick-figure Anthony Caro sculpture, it is quite an extravagant composition. The Roman Bath vaulted ceilings are the point of interest for this writing with their 24-carat gilding they both weigh down spatially and lift up visually, a neat trick. Of all the decorative and historic possibilities available the simplicity of this solution and the sensuality of the materials is all quite beautiful.

GLASS VAULTED CEILING
HAROLD WASHINGTON LIBRARY CENTER (1992)

When doing research for my books I frequent room 300 Art and Architecture in the Main Branch of the New York City Public Library. To get to this little room you have to walk through the magnificent Rose Reading Room. First pass a guard checkpoint, then push past the tourists and their jousting selfie sticks, then a long walk past huge wooden desks seating young people using free Wi-Fi for European soccer games, cable TV, Zooming buddies, almost anything but reading the non-circulating library books. The glorious neoclassical space (52-foot ceiling height

78-foot width and 297-foot length) always struck me as like being inside the head of the city with all its random stupidity and possible brilliance. The sky blue and rose tinted clouds in the ceiling murals are the escape hatch for the exploding madness and power of words.

But, how is it that the Harold Washington Library Center in Chicago does not have a main reading room? The symmetric escalators, the low ceiling typical floors, the open plan reading and stack areas seem to have a suburban shopping mall vibe. You just keep wandering to get to the big room where it all happens and then it never happens.

There is no main reading room but there are some rooftop volumes that speak volumes about possibilities. There is the wonderful and enchanting Winter Garden Court on the ninth floor (ceiling height also a solid 52 feet) designed by the architect Hammond Beeby and Babka, designer Thomas Beeby. Here a symmetric cross vaulted skylight gives the climax to the long passage through the building. But where are the reading desks in this noble room? Where are the readers and their tattered books and shiny laptops? Why does it smell like cappuccino?

Maybe for exiting reasons, maybe for security reasons, maybe for money reasons, this is not the main reading room but basically an airy rentable party space.

Yet, the vaulted ceiling is magnificent in its over-articulated steel truss, diagonal bracing and turn of the last century sort of way. This is not the head and brains of the city but more like a Victorian botanical greenhouse fantasy for tea and cakes. I sit here and look up into the glass vault to the gloomy Chicago winter sky with the already dirty snow falling and wonder if I could be evil and sneak a book up here to read?

METAL TRELLIS VAULTED CEILING
JAY PRITZKER MUSIC PAVILION (2004)

There is the Architect-Speak term the "Bilbao Effect" which refers to the Guggenheim Museum in Bilbao, Spain designed by the architectural firm Frank O. Gehry and Associates. The phrase connects to the use of a star architect and a spectacular vision that when built drives the tourist industry to ecstatic profits and acclaim. Chicago City Hall wanted that thing called the "Bilbao Effect" and the Pritzker Music Pavilion, in Millennium Park, is the result.

It is the ultimate architectural stage set: a false facade without a building supporting it or a Potemkin proscenium arch for a musical puppet show. The structure consists of a set of curvilinear aluminum ribbon panels with stainless steel cover sheets supported by a system of triangulated steel tube trusses with the entire framework backed up against the blank party wall of the Harris Theater for Music and Dance.

But for our interests it is the trellis and lawn that is relevant to our argument, for there is a really wacky woven vault of steel tubes that attach to fat, 6-foot diameter, cylinders at the aisles and provide the sophisticated sound system for the musical performances. The trellis far exceeds what is required to support the little speaker sets; it is the glory of a parabolic vault that does not just represent the sky but has transformed into the sky. Bravo! Felissimo! Maestro! Encore!

Lobby - 190 S. LaSalle St. (1986) - Architect: John Burgee Architects
with Philip Johnson - Designer: Philip Johnson

Harold Washington Library Center (1992) - Winter Garden - floor nine
Architect: Hamond Beeby and Babka - Designer: Thomas Beeby

The Jay Pritzker Pavilion (2004) - Lakeshore Dr. and Randolph St. - Architect: Frank O. Gehry & Assoc.

THE IMPOSSIBILITY OF ADDITIONS

THE ZEITGEIST VS THE CONTEXT

What would seem to be a straight forward problem of expanding an existing structure is fraught with deep psychological conflicts for the contemporary architect. This is because, even for the smallest addition, architects must confront where they stand on the issue of the immediacy of the Zeitgeist versus the historic continuity of the Context.

The argument for the "Context" states that we have an obligation to establish a link with our past and extend the scale, materials and style of our most beloved buildings and neighborhoods. The architects who can't understand this are destructive egomaniacs or just plain evil. Unfortunately, the context as an idea can be used to justify the most banal and retardataire buildings.

The other strategy states that we can only build true to our own time and a gesture toward duplicating the style, materials or forms of the past is a moral failure, where the offending architect is obviously mentally deficient. If you have to attach something to a nice old building, you don't confuse everyone by blurring where the old starts and the new begins. Some have labeled this attitude as following the "Zeitgeist," a term that can be roughly translated from the German as the "Spirit of Today." Unfortunately, the definition of the "today" is a bit impoverished and additions along these lines are mostly big gridded glass boxes indelicately attached to smaller historic masonry structures.

Chicago has some of the better quality additions done in both manners.

ZEITGEIST – ADLER PLANETARIUM ADDITION

The art deco Adler Planetarium (1930) and its glass addition (1999) are a great example of the Zeitgeist addition concept. The planetarium is a twelve sided figure (twelve zodiac sculptures on its facade) that supports a half spherical dome, which is the planetarium's spherical theater screen projecting above the roof line. The building is clad in polished, red/black granite that adds to its distinctive character. It is a perfect object building, floating in isolation on the lakefront, detached from any other structure. One of the additions to the building in 1999, by the architects Lohan Associates, is a gridded glass truncated cone connecting to the stone box with a few adjustments. Dirk Lohan has sympathetically elaborated the geometry by making the addition a half circle in plan and conical in form. So that from above the assembly looks like two abstract geometric shapes interlocked in a love fest. As always you must look at the edges of architecture to understand it completely. The addition at its western edge articulates the cone shape in a slice that results in a set of blank stone/metal triangles that tries to be a sympathetic elevation to the geometry of the main building. Luckily, the lake view is east and opposite the main entry so the addition has little conflict with that part of the old. What makes this addition "Zeitgeisty" is the extreme geometry and the complete glass cladding that screams: I am modern mister! What makes it tolerable is its slightly smaller size than the main structure, its limited intrusion of the main entry facade and its matching of the original's severe geometry.

CONTEXT — 222 NORTH LASALLE STREET

To contrast the Zeitgeist attitude let's look another addition but this time with the idea relating to the "Context." The 30-story office building at 222 North LaSalle Street (1927) was originally called the Builder's Building, but the Depression emptied it of that business and it became just another address. Designed by Big Dan Burnham's successor firm Graham Anderson Probst & White, it has a tripartite division of a limestone base, a white terra cotta body and topping off with a colonnade/cornice combo. The building has a simplified neoclassical order remnant from the 1893 Columbian Exposition "White City." It might be called a generic Chicago "Classical Box" with the exception of a rather dazzling multi-floor interior lobby space that goes beyond the demands of real estate marketing.

The addition (including a new hotel) of 1986 by SOM takes the material and vertical rhythmical order of the facade and simply duplicates it like extending a wallpaper pattern in the next westernmost lot. The copy is not exact for the neoclassical columns and recessed floors at the top of the first get flattened out and simplified in the second. The architects go even further in blurring the difference between the two by installing four additional new floors to the old building as a sloped glass mansard that matches the addition. The corner window pattern of the old is duplicated as a similar surround on the new as if the addition is a smaller version of the original. From a distance across the river the distinction of the two is clear but the asymmetry of the new assembly is a wonderful balance between the original and the new.

A DIFFERENT SOLUTION
MINIATURIZATION — CHICAGO BOARD OF TRADE

There is a third option in the debate on additions and one that distorts the idea of context to have the architect not just reuse the base building's general materials and forms but to reproduce the entire original structure in miniature. This may sound a little strange but it has been used before and in Chicago. Some have called this technique a pseudo scientific name: "Critical Scale Distortion."

The first example of this type is the 1980 addition to the great 1930s art deco skyscraper, the Chicago Board of Trade. The architect Helmut Jahn of C.F. Murphy used a neutral grid of glass curtain wall but shaped it into a duplicate of the pyramidal roof of the original. He went as far as making a matching sculptural object at the top. Where the original building has a hauntingly beautiful abstract sculpture of Ceres, Goddess of Grain, by the artist Robert Storrs, symbolic of the agricultural trading below, the addition's top sculpture is a stepped octagon which represents the trading pits and the Board of Trade's logo. At a distance this looks strangely like the hood ornament of a Mercedes-Benz Limousine, a symbol the traders below fully understand. I wish that instead of the logo the artwork could have been a statue of Persephone, the tragic daughter of Ceres, whose fate would remind the traders of the changing fortunes of the market. The smaller height of the addition gives a sympathetic stepped massing of the total assembly. If the Jahn design inflects the typical modern Zeitgeist gridded glass addition into something more in context of the original it is still reluctant to commit to a continuity of any materials or style of the art deco building.

POSSIBLE ADDITIONS- MINIATURIZATION
MUSEUM OF SCIENCE AND UNITY TEMPLE

The second example of miniaturization takes the Museum of Science and Industry and its original plan, the 1893 Palace of Fine Arts, that shows the main building's cross axis with a dome organization and sees it duplicated in a symmetric order of two smaller pavilions with the same cross axis and much smaller domes. Although the entire three pieces were built at the same time, it still shows a charming potential solution for expansions and additions. The side buildings are low enough that they don't compete with the central structure, and their facades are an amazing simplification of the central temple form, but in my mind they can be simply seen as offsprings holding hands with the central parent.

The third example requires a bit of imagination of the reader in that it proposes that the Unity Temple in Oak Park (1908) by Frank Lloyd Wright, which has an adjacent meeting house, could be an excellent example of an addition by way of miniaturization of the main hall. This also ignores the fact that they were both built at the same time. However, you can see that the main facade of the small meeting house with its blank walls, ornamented columns and cantilevered cornice makes a really good shrunken down version of the main building. By necessity the stair towers of the temple become reduced to closets in the meeting hall. Obviously, the two don't entirely match for the main hall is a large cube and the meeting house is a smaller rectangular box but the image of a smaller twin is there and an interesting solution to the building's layout.

There are a few other examples of miniaturization in Chicago. Frank Lloyd Wright proposed a half scale prairie home for the kid's play-house at the unbuilt McCormick residence design of 1907. I truly love this caprice because it reminds me that Wright's second son, John Lloyd Wright, did a wonderful and famous toy design, Lincoln Logs in 1918, that is my best example of miniaturization (the product was first manufactured in Chicago). It is shown here in its first packaging box, along with the architect's delightful cubic font, drawn by T-square and triangle. In its simplest definition what is miniaturization but the honor of being seen as a toy?

The addition by miniaturization is not a generic solution for the problem of expanding existing structures, but for my opinion it is a unique and fascinating variation on the debate of how additions can be made and then extended to a larger sense how the city grows and what that looks like.

Adler Planetarium (1930) - 1300 S. Lake Shore Dr. - Architect: Ernest Grunsfeld
Addition (1999) - Architect: Lohan Assoc.

Postcard: Builders Building (1927) - 222 N. LaSalle St.
Architect: Graham Anderson Probst & White

222 N. LaSalle St. (1927)
Architect: Graham Anderson
Probst & White
Addition: (1986) Architect: SOM

Chicago Board of Trade Building (1930) - 141 W. Jackson Blvd.- Architect: Holabird & Root
Addition (1980) - Architect: Murphy/Jahn

Maquette of Ceres sculpture (31-foot tall)
Artist: John Storrs (1930)

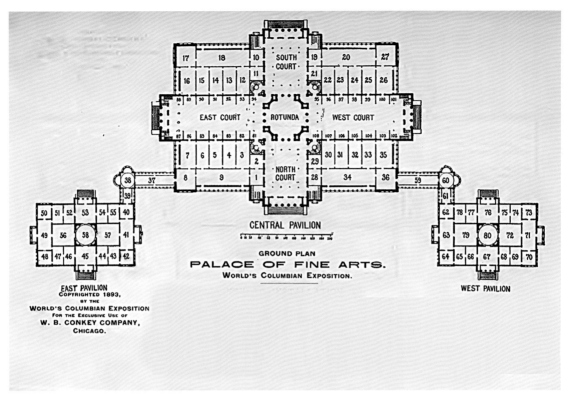

Plan of the Palace of Fine Arts (1893), later the Museum of Science and Industry

Postcard: (circa 1930) Museum of Science and Industry showing the two symmetrical pavilions and linking corridors

Unity Temple (1908) - 875 W. Lake St., Oak Park- Architect: Frank Lloyd Wright - West Elevation

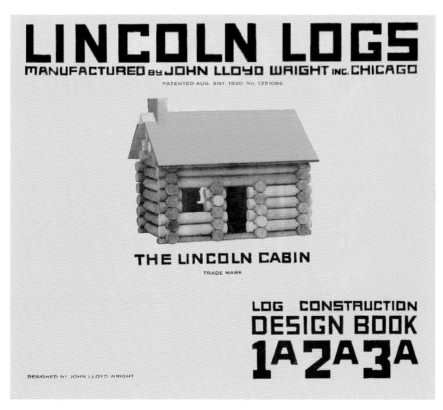

Original packaging of Lincoln Logs Toy (1918) - Designer: John Lloyd Wright

FUTURE MODERN

VCNA concrete plant is located near the intersection of Chicago Ave. and Halsted St. The industrial imagery of silos, sky ramps and opaque rusting towers are the imaginary Sci-Fi city of the future that never looked so good.

ARCHITECTURE PARLANTE
THE SPEAKING ARCHITECTURE

NORMAN FOSTER AND OSCAR MAYER

The term *Architecture Parlante* is not part of the everyday vocabulary of architects. But it is a useful term for our world of overkill advertising and omnipresent pop art. It simply means "The Speaking Architecture," its use is in the extreme symbolic development of the function of a building through its form. The classic example is the eighteenth century architect, Jean-Jacques Lequeu, doing a rendering titled *Southern View of Cow's Stable on a Cool Meadow* with that hay loft building in the shape of a cow.

This idea has been used by a number of famous architects: Raymond Hood, of the Tribune Tower fame, did a refrigerator showroom building (1920s) in the shape of, you guessed it, a refrigerator. Its relevance was revived by the post modern architect Robert Venturi who based his criticism of the aggressive form making of 1960s architects by using the Flanders, New York roadside poultry sales pavilion "The Duck" as mockery (mock duck?). And, of course, every World's Fair has pavilions in the shape of its product; my favorite in Chicago's Century of Progress International Exposition of 1933 is the Havoline Motor Oil Company Building as a multistory thermometer, designed by the artist Alfonso Iannelli. Please note that neon tubes were used as a substitute for the normal sized thermometer's mercury indicator.

Also, there is the famous 1922 *Architectural Competition for the Chicago Tribune Tower* which among its 260 submitted designs had a few that are easily in the line of *Architecture Parlante*. And to add even more entries, a separate revisit of the competition was done in 1980, as part of the post modern explosion in Chicago by the Lennon and McCartney of the Chicago architect scene: Stanley Tigerman and Stuart Cohen. You may remember that Lennon was the mean one and McCartney was the nice one.

The most famous of the first competition (more than the winner) was the work by the Austrian architect Adolf Loos with his tower in the shape of an ancient Greek fluted Tuscan column with a real column capital as the cornice. This design speaks to a sarcastic and literal interpretation of Louis Sullivan's definition of the "Chicago Tall Building" as composed as a base, shaft and capital. Let's not forget that as a young man Loos came to visit Chicago for the 1893 Columbian Exposition and paid for his stay with a grueling dish washing job, maybe after that he just did not like the City.

The *Architecture Parlante* proposal from the 1980 competition that most amuses is the *Tommy Gun Tower* by the Dutch architect Hans Tupker (who died in 2015). Here is a high-tech tower of multiple diagonal bracing and angular plan that is shaped into a vertical machine gun from the Al Capone era. It is both a post modern pastiche and the unfortunate reality that Chicago's reputation in the world is still tied to the gangster movies from the late 1940s. Perhaps director Christopher Nolan (who spent his teen years in Evanston) with his Batman movies, which were shot in the Chicago, will change the image of the City to be a home for a "better class of criminals."

APPLE MICHIGAN AVENUE STORE

Chicago has many building size signs but few buildings in the shape of its product. However there is one that is most prominent, the Apple Michigan Avenue store of 2020 designed by the London architects Foster + Partners. Specifically the half curved edge of the flat carbon fiber roof matches the curved edge, or bezel, of the Apple product, the iPhone. Also, the rectangular proportion of the roof is very similar to the iPhone case. This roof design was previously developed by Foster for a project of hillside houses in Norway (2015) where the top roof shape was duplicated in a mirrored curved cantilevered floor shape, making it even more an iPhone twin.

WIENERMOBILE

The other Chicago example of built *Architecture Parlante* is the beloved Oscar Mayer Wienermobile. To clarify, I am not confusing Oscar Mayer (Chicago meat man) with Oscar Niemeyer (Brazilian modern architect). This is obviously a rather rude analogy to compare Sir Norman Foster's super-serious high-tech design to a big blood-red fiberglass hot dog on a mustard yellow car body bun, but I believe it has value in explaining this idea.

The Wienermobile is an advertising gimmick that the Oscar Mayer Foods Company (based in Chicago) first produced in 1936, designed by the nephew of the owner, Carl G. Mayer. Over the years the W-mobile fleet has expanded to over six and is used in good will publicity events. I am not saying that the Wienermobile is the logical successor of the eighteenth century "Visionary Architects" of the French Revolution but that it has a place in the story of how design is seen, communicated and enjoyed by many Chicagoans. *Architecture Parlante* is rare for Chicago, but still a powerful design tool for our time.

I find the hot dog theme song, that every Chicago expatriate knows, played as a slow ballad extremely sad and haunting:

> Oh I wish I was an Oscar Mayer Wiener
> that is what I truly want to be
> Cuz if I were an Oscar Meyer Wiener
> everyone would be in love with me

Wienermobile - First version 1936 by General Body Co., Chicago - latest version (1988) - Designer: Brooks Stevens

Postcard: Havoline Motor Oil Building Pavilion at the 1933 Chicago World's Fair. The building is in the shape of an operating multistory thermometer. Neon tubes were the substitute for the standard thermometer's mercury. Designer: Alfonso Iannelli

Chicago Tribune Tower Competition (1922)
Architect: Adolf Loos

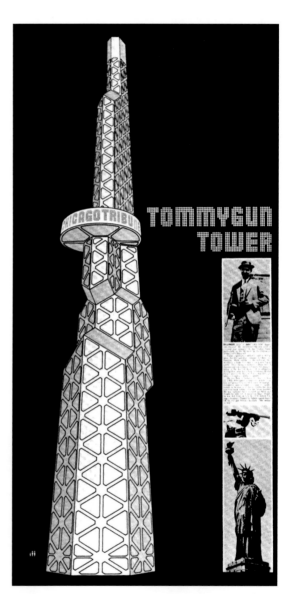

Late Entries- Chicago Tribune Tower Competition (1980)
Tommy Gun Tower - Architect: Hans Tupker

Apple Michigan Ave. (2020) - 401 N. Michigan Ave.- Architect: Foster + Partners

Apple iPhone advertisement showing the curved edge bezel

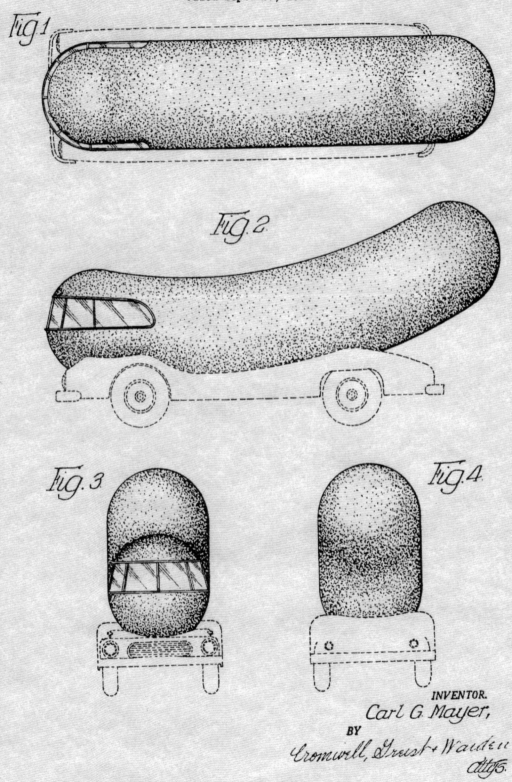

Fig.1

Fig.2

Fig.3

Fig.4

INVENTOR.

Carl G. Mayer,

BY

Cromwell, Greist + Warden

Attys.

INTERIORS AS SCI-FI STYLE

HELMUT JAHN, FLASH GORDON AND MR. MACHINE

Here I am using the image of the future as the one with a technologically advanced science fiction chrome shine and not the dark dystopian rubble and ruins kind. I find that the architect firm JAHN has done some wonderful wild and wacky futuristic designs under the protective cover of being straight no-nonsense high-tech architecture and therefore avoiding any criticism. I first heard of the designer Helmut Jahn of C.F. Murphy Associates in 1980 after the construction of the smooth and silvery Xerox Center building at 55 Monroe Street was completed. *Newsweek* dubbed the designer as the "Flash Gordon" of the architecture world in November 1982. This is a perfect "man on the street" Chicago take on what other places would call High Modern, High-Tech or simply Future Modern.

The three interiors that I am proposing as the best of Chicago Futuristic Sci-Fi is the underground pedestrian tunnel at the United Airlines Terminal 1 (1987) in O'Hare Airport, the Joe and Rika Mansueto Library Reading Room (2011) and the West Campus Utility Plant (2010), both at the University of Chicago. All were designed by the JAHN firm and all are more than big mechanical objects; they illustrate a variety of influences from cinema, surrealism, racing cars, spaceships (NASA Lunar Lander) and toys.

UNITED AIRLINES TERMINAL 1 UNDERGROUND PEDESTRIAN TUNNEL

The O'Hare Airport pedestrian tunnel experience is an unmedicated psychedelic trip of floating in a dream-like state on a moving sidewalk. The flashing, syncopated and flickering colored argon gas tube assembly is a work by the California/Canadian artist Michael Hayden titled *Sky's the Limit*. For heightened cinemagraphic effect it was coordinated with a special eerie electronic music composition by William Kraft, which unfortunately was replaced with the crowd pleasing *Rhapsody in Blue*.

I cannot help to note that the movement and light show is so much like the ending sequence in Stanley Kubrick's movie *2001: a Space Odyssey* (1968), it is such an incredible match. I asked the artist about this possible connection and he dismissed it as a cute idea.

If we look carefully at the central artwork we can see that it takes the even rhythm of the undulating, back-lit side walls as the start of its geometry. The first argon gas tubes are a single line that matches the wall curves and then increases in its frequency with multiple bent pieces that gives a frantic concentration of visual activity.

The lighting program moves this activity along a single direction to create movement and a distorted perspective. The angular forms of the lighting tubes gives the effect of a solid three dimensionality that would have been less effective if the tubes were laid out flat on the mirrored ceiling.

The comparison of the light sculpture to a section of a film is very pretentious but I still believe it has value. The movie section I am referencing is the long scene of

Amazing Archigram 4 (1968)
produced by the British architect
group Archigram

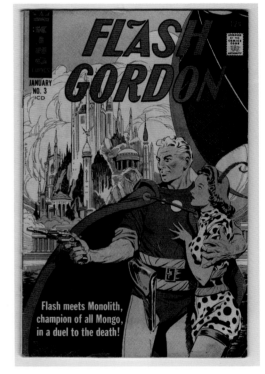

Flash Gordon comic book - January no. 3, 1967

United Airlines Terminal 1 - underground pedestrian tunnel (1987) O'Hare Airport
Architect: Murphy/Jahn- Artist: Michael Hayden, *Sky's the Limit*.

Artist interpretation of climactic scene of movie, *2001: A Space Odyssey*

the swirling colors noting the passage through the *Star Gate* in the movie *2001*. This special effect was developed by Douglas Trumbull (who got no credit in the Oscar award to the film's effects) with an invention called a "slit scan" machine that has been explained and diagrammed elsewhere. What is so wonderful about this visual sequence is how spatial the slit scan segments are. The movie and the sculpture unite in my mind to form the perfect cinematic city.

JOE AND RIKA MANSUETO LIBRARY READING ROOM

The other interior of note is the reading room in the Mansueto Library pavilion at the University of Chicago. An ovoid domed glass house (120 feet x 240 feet) that is separated from the rectangular limestone Regenstein main library building, designed by Walter Netsch of SOM in 1970, so that you enter from a ground level bridge (that is in itself very high-tech). The addition has an amazing fully robotic book retrieval system in its multi-level basement, making an easy analogy of the Teamsters "Morlocks" below and an Ivy League "Eloi" above from the novel *The Time Machine*, a sci-fi master/servant utopia.

One of the things to observe in the interior (the University does give tours) is the proportion of the metal frame to the coated glass. How much is solid and how much is void? I think you will agree there is a surprisingly lot of solid on the inside. There is a delicate balance in a glass box design between giving a feeling of enclosure and opening transparency to the outside. It is my observation that there is so much metal frame/structure that you don't see much of the outside and the real value of the room is in the quality of natural light for reading (or for the distraction of glare on your laptop screen).

To make a close reading of any architecture you try to observe the edges of things. And in this library the edge of how the building hits the ground is quite strange. The shallow dome rests on a diagonal concrete flange and then is surrounded by a ring of suburban hedge planting. It seems somewhat of a pedestrian solution. But in a quick reference to the online published hand sketches of Jahn you can see that this area was originally a slanted glass base that allowed the public to glimpse into the basement mechanical workings that move up and down, round and round in the robotic book retrieval.

WEST CAMPUS COMBINED UTILITY PLANT

Only two blocks west of the Mansueto Library is the West Campus Combined Utility Plant (2010) on Maryland Avenue. Here Jahn produced another glass box as the ultimate high-tech toy. The multistory mechanical plant facade is clear glass so that a passer-by can admire and wonder at the tangle of multi-colored pipes and conduits that make up the guts of the building; boilers are red, chillers are blue and pumps are green. The display of color-coded mechanical systems is a High-Tech trope that can be seen in multiple futuristic buildings like the Centre Pompidou in Paris. The only disappointment I have is that nothing visible is moving; no spinning counterweights, no pumping pistons and no flashing lights on a visible control panel.

Exterior-University of Chicago – Joe and Rika Mansueto Library reading room (2011) - 1100 E. 57 th St. - Architect: JAHN

Interior-University of Chicago - Joe and Rika Mansueto Library reading room (2011) - 1100 E. 57 th St. - Architect: JAHN

Here is where I make an analogy from the building to the toy "Mr. Machine" (1960), as an exemplar of High-Tech before the word was coined. Only 18-inches tall, it was a plastic walking robot that had its colored moving gears visible through its clear plastic body. It was made by Ideal Toys and designed by the Chicago firm Marvin Glass & Associates, the idea of a building as a glass box that opens up its mechanical workings is a dream of early modernist architects perhaps connected to their childhood toys.

As a small child and a great lover of destroying plastic toys; I remember making a successful effort to nag my father to drive by the Marvin Glass Toy Studio on the near north side of the city. The building no longer exists, but it was a solid limestone-clad, two-story, perfect cube without any windows and a hidden entrance (could I have misremembered it?). Maximum security from industrial espionage and maximum paranoia of Mr. Glass was the reason for this opaque building. Marvin Glass died in 1974 and in 1976 a disgruntled employee brought a gun to work, then opened fire in the studio, killing two and wounding five of the staff. Santa's workshop it was not. For the child in me it was the ultimate building to hold the most precious secrets of the universe. A Pandora's Box of creepy commercialism and corporate exploitation of children's dreams, I loved all of it.

Helmut Jahn (who died in 2021) named his racing sailboat "Flash Gordon," so I think calling him "Mr. Machine" would be an understandable compliment, indeed.

Note: The influence of mechanical toys on the aesthetics of High-Tech architects has been written about by others. The architect Norman Foster has acknowledged the importance of Meccano Erector Sets in inspiring him in his youth and at the 1980s London office of the architect Richard Rogers there was an industrial design group subleasing space and doing model mock-ups of "Transformer" toys (plastic cars that twisted into a special robot shapes), which were on display for the entire architect's office to enjoy.

Not to be ignored is the sci-fi inspired fantasy drawings of the British 1960s architectural group called Archigram. Is that the 1963 DC Comics *Mystery in Space,* superhero Adam Strange on the cover of their issue no. 4, self-titled magazine, I wonder?

University of Chicago - West Campus Combined Utility Plant (2010) - 5617 S. Maryland Ave.- Architect: JAHN

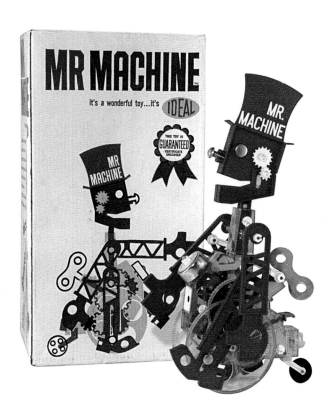

Mr. Machine toy (1960)
IDEAL TOY CO.
Designer: Marvin Glass & Assoc.

UNBUILT CHICAGO, THE FUTURE IS NOT FORGOTTEN

There are some amazing futuristic designs proposed for sites in Chicago that never got to the start of construction. But that does not mean that the developers, architects and schemers gave up on their discarded dreams. In the world of Architect-Speak there is an entire section of "Paper Architecture" which gives honor to works never built and if these objects have a strong idea behind them they might have a longer life span then buildings that were actually constructed.

The foremost example that comes to mind is the unbuilt curved cornered apartment building for Rush & Delaware by the Bowman Brothers Architects (1930). The historian Philip Johnson included projects by these Chicago architects in his seminal MoMA exhibit, *The International Style* (1932) and then the architect Philip Johnson later used their designs for the inspiration of some of his own constructions as the Metropolitan Condominiums at 181 East 90th Street, New York City (2004).

THE TOWER OF BABEL
MILE HIGH ILLINOIS

The idea of the tallest building in the world is more than a priapism and masturbatory fantasy; it is a major cultural component of late capitalism. It has been many years since the Willis (Sears) Tower lost its crowning glory to the Malaysian Petronas Towers (1998) as the world's tallest building. And when the Chicago architect Adrian Smith of SOM designed the current "big boy" champ, the Burj Khalifa in Dubai, a number of articles compared the super slender "spike" to the 1956 fantasy tower designed by Frank Lloyd Wright, that he called the Mile High Illinois. What can you say about this crazy 89-year-old guy doing an absurd publicity stunt to show he was still the Master Architect and could get it up? It is certainly one of the most famous "Paper Architecture" projects that he had produced.

The Mile High project's name came from its audacious building height of 5,280 feet (528 floors) and with the addition of the antenna it arrives at the total height of 5,706 feet. As a comparison the current tallest Burj is only a pitiful 2,722 feet to the tip of its antenna, making it less than half of Wright's wet dream. But both have a modified triangular plan with the logic of having the structure of the towers based on tripod stability from three bearing walls. The Wright design has many more Sci-Fi effects than the almost practical Burj, for example at one point a set of (atomic powered) elevators pop out of the building's sloped and receding enclosure to become glass observation elevator tubes of the future, NICE!

The fact that no one rushed to try to build the Mile High Illinois is to be expected, but the "money shot" of Wright at Chicago's Sherman House Hotel conference room standing in front of the 30-foot tall unfolded rendering is one of the grandest ego-maniacal nightmares that I can imagine.

Apartment project (1930)
Rush & Delaware Streets
Architect: Bowman Brothers

102

Chicago Spire at the Chicago River
(2007) - 2,000 ft tall (609 m)
400 N. Lake Shore Dr.
Architect: Santiago Calatrava

Mile-High Illinois skyscraper for Chicago (1957)
528 floors - top of building 5,280 foot (1,609 m)
top of antenna 5,706 foot (1,739 m)
Architect: Frank Lloyd Wright

CHICAGO SPIRE

Santiago Calatrava qualifies for the term "Starchitect" as the engineer and architect of some absolutely wild bridges, train stations, museums and other futuristically styled buildings. His work in Chicago for the 2007 Chicago Spire project continued with the mathematically distorted forms that he has used elsewhere. For Chicago it was a helical spiral that continued to a tapered point at the top of its 2,000-feet-tall pinnacle. The building qualified as a Megatall Tower by slightly going over the 600 meter (1,968 foot) finish line. The project went through some amazingly disastrous economic problems that led to its cancellation in 2014, which we will not examine (boring!).

To concentrate on the object at hand; the Spire is important to Chicago because there is nothing like it in the city. The obvious rectangular logic might be bent slightly as in the cylinders of Marina City Towers or the irregular curved balconies of the block Aqua, but Calatrava moves form making into another level of complexity. And as a separate point the location of the now dead tower was at the mouth of the Chicago River making it an incredibly important addition to the skyline, relocating the visible center of the city in its northern march. The initial designs show an isolated "drill bit" separated from the city by a small park, river and lakefront; obviously Calatrava failed to consider how to land his alien space ship. The isolation and juxtaposition of dramatic designs is part of the argument in the next section.

THE UNLOVED MONUMENT

Both of the following two unbuilt structures represent an imaginary idealized world that would have nested into a piece of the larger and messier City of Chicago. If built on their original sites they would have been totally alien to their immediate surroundings. But maybe that's the point.

THE LUCAS MUSEUM OF NARRATIVE ART

George Lucas, the creator of the Star Wars cinematic empire, wanted to establish a museum that would engage one idea: the enduring power of narrative art.

The determined Lucas presented his new building for a site in San Francisco (rejected) and then in Chicago (rejected) and was finally accepted and built in Los Angeles (2023). Building renderings for all three cities were designed by Chinese architect Ma Yansong of MAD Architects, who was presented by Lucas as a "futuristic architect ... giving us a building of the twenty-first century." The Chicago building was a sloped, volcano-like form that spread out in a curved flowing lava perimeter with the volcano's throat as a cylindrical top observation platform. The problem was the existing parking lot site was at the edge of the lakefront on public land. The mantra of the lakefront as free and open forever was too legally compelling for this proposal to advance, but I think the jarring appearance of the white stone-clad anomaly in a city of conservative dark grids was also part of its downfall. It was intentionally meant to stand out as separate to its surroundings. To fight against the accepted opinion of all, I find the building to be unusual and is something that is new

Lucas Museum of Narrative Art (2014)

Rendering of unrealized design for the Lucas Museum of Narrative Art in Chicago
by MAD Architects; courtesy of the Lucas Museum of Narrative Art

and challenging in every way to Chicago's design culture. So for those reasons alone it should have been built. The city is either constantly changing or it is continually dying; an exchange of a parking lot for a unique white sculptural monument would not have destroyed the lakefront and its sanctity. The city and its citizens failed in imagination and confidence in rejecting this possible "future." But then again, perhaps what defines Chicago now is its simultaneous decay and grandeur.

THE NEW CITY HALL

This project presentation is meant to be an amusing conjecture on the combined histories of Burnham's Plan of Chicago (1906) and the development of the expressway system in the city during the 1950s.

When Burnham developed his Chicago Plan he synthesized the disciplines of transportation, sanitation, politics and architecture to make a proposal to take the booming city into the next 100 years of development; little of that plan was actually implemented. But the dazzling panoramic perspectives by the artist Jules Guerin gave the report a very unscientific slant toward the lush watercolor imagery of wide boulevards, expansive parks and neoclassical civic monuments all looking exactly like an American tourist's dream of Paris, France.

For a 2020 Chicago Architectural Club competition to comment on Burnham's plan, I proposed in a post-card image that the Burnham imaginary Parisian New Chicago City Hall be located in its original position on the near west side which is now the Circle Traffic Interchange. This area was ceremoniously titled the Jane Byrne Interchange during its major renovation in 2014. I ask you, who in their right mind would want to have the most congested roadway intersection in America named after them? This monstrous full four square city blocks of swooping elevated roadway badly unites the Eisenhower, Dan Ryan and Kennedy expressways.

So to delicately place the redrawn rendering of the 1906 City Hall over this spaghetti of roadway makes a surreal juxtaposition of design philosophies, urban planning concepts and exaggerated notions of American grandeur. The multilane roads zoom through the ground floor monumental Beaux Arts entries and pass under and out of the structure. History is presented as a series of overlapping layers each visible and dynamic. I find it all very kinetic and exciting.

Also, let us not forget that nearby the incredible 1921 building, The Central Post Office, which straddles Congress Street like a fortress wall, a lumbering giant and a remnant from Le Corbusier's 1930s modern urban planning schemes. The Post Office building also lets the flow of traffic go through its structure like the fantasy New City Hall.

Both the Museum of Narrative Arts and the New City Hall attempt to shock and disorient the viewer by the extreme contrast to their environments. But I would argue that this is one solution of many in the constantly built urban collage called the City of Chicago.

Postcard: New Chicago City Hall
Original location in Chicago
Plan (1906) is now the west side
expressway interchange
Architect: D. H .Burnham & Co.
Fantasy Postcard
by Christian Bjone (2020)

Postcard: Central Post Office (1931)
433 W. Van Buren St.
Architects: Graham Anderson Probst & White
The building has Congress St. running
under and through its center.

THE TOTAL NODAL MODAL INTERCHANGE

TWO TRANSPORTATION PAVILIONS

The title of this essay refers to a 1970's Urban Planning term with rhyming cadence that notes a spot where various transportation systems meet up and merge: trains meet planes and buses meet subways. No one is so optimistic on making the city work anymore so the term has fallen out of favor. But there are two Chicago transportation pavilions that I think are worthy of acclaim.

BP GAS STATION

The massive curved steel frame of this gas station is an incredible delight; rarely is an engineering structure so evocative of a four-legged muscular crouching animal waiting to pounce. It is over-structured with four interior columns and completely sculptural, located on an open triangular site with the diagonal thrust of Clark Street that seems to push it forward in frozen speed. It may not be the best gas station design in the world but it is an eccentric visual manipulation of an inert steel frame for all to enjoy.

CTA BELMONT STATION

This elaborate entry is for the underground blue line Belmont El train station with a point of connection to the CTA bus lines (77 & 80). It presents an open 68-foot cantilevered structure that is an elaborate flourish very much the opposite of the BP gas station. Here at the Belmont stop the steel acts a dramatic projecting form that gives lightness to the entire assembly of hollow steel frames. The addition of curves and blue colored polycarbonate panels adds to another animalistic metaphor of dragonfly wings. It seems almost counterintuitive that you move from this light and delightful canopy to a frumpy, dirty old CTA bus and not into an equally light dirigible airship, Captain Nemo's submarine or a zooming World's Fair monorail.

BP Gas Station (1971) - 1647 N. LaSalle Blvd.- Architect: George W. Terp Jr.

CTA Belmont Station (2019) - N. Kimball Ave. and W. Belmont Ave. - Architect: Ross Barney Architects

THE GESAMTKUNSTWERK, TOTAL WORK OF ART

THE ARTIST AS ARCHITECT
EDGAR MILLER AND THEASTER GATES

There is an overused Architect-Speak phrase, a loan word from Germany, "The Gesamtkunstwerk" which is a mouthful that translates as "the total work of art" and in the world of contemporary architecture it means that the architects designed everything in sight. It also can mean that the author of a building's design might not be an architect but an artist whose scope of work is complete from facade to door knobs. These two Chicago artists have reestablished a little known tradition of innovative residential renovation that goes way beyond any *Flip This House* TV show cliché and moves into the stunningly beautiful and profound.

EDGAR MILLER

The 1930s were a tough time for artists and everyone else; there was a desire to expand beyond the commercial limitations of the fine art world and address crushing social problems. This took the form of the WPA mural movement and other political engagement of the arts, which created an environment where a wide range of expression was accepted and explored. I would like to think that the incredible work of the artist and designer Edgar Miller (1899–1993) produced in various art forms; advertising posters, furniture design, product design and house embellishments that were part of that era's best Chicago work.

To see the few houses that he remade is quite a treat, most are still private, but the R.W. Glasner Studio is open through specific tours by the Edgar Miller Legacy, therefore that it is the only one that I will review. The Studio is located in a complex of other studios in the back of the courtyard entered at the red-orange door at 1734 North Wells Street. It was originally designed as a weekend party house and I will describe the first floor living room only and its emphasis on certain motifs and surfaces. My first point is that not every surface is covered in ornament or pattern and that there is a selective limitation that Miller uses to enhance his ornament. The most dominant form is a motif pattern of diamonds and by extension diagonal elements, this is seen in the stained glass windows, the edge molding of all of the ceiling beams/joists and it is even seen in the wood cut-out heating grilles under the windows. The second item I wish to draw your attention to the general color arrangement seen in the ceiling panel colors of a dominant red-orange followed by, in decreasing order, brown and then blue-gray and thin cream edges (all within the sympathetic shades of brown in the wood floor and staircase) the total effect is as controlled as a stage set. The profusion of carved animals appear everywhere (so many weasels!) and are a delight in themselves. This room is not a crazy explosion of ornament for its own sake but an amazingly controlled and calculated color environment like being inside a beating heart. Make the effort to get a reservation to be transported back into another world where art was its lifeblood.

R. W. Glasner Studio (1928-1970) -1734 N. Wells St.- ground floor living room - Renovation by Artist: Edgar Miller

Edgar Miller, circa 1940

Theaster Gates, 2015

R. W. Glasner Studio (1928-1970) -1734 N. Wells St. - Entry- Renovation by Artist: Edgar Miller

THEASTER GATES

There is a recent trend for contemporary artists to expand their vision to encompass more than the tradition mediums of painting and sculpture to entire environments. The term "Social Practice" defines an area of work that engages various media, political topics and social interaction. The Chicago artist Theaster Gates would be the best representative of that attack on opening up the art world's definitions. Gates produces numerous amazing works in monumental ceramic, wood constructs (the series on monstrous Shoe Shine Chairs) and other assemblies, but I will limit myself to two renovated buildings in his Dorchester Projects. The first is the "Archive House," a renovated gabled house and the "Stony Island Arts Bank" a refurbished neoclassical bank. For entry and times of operations see the Dorchester Arts + Housing Collaborative (1456 East 70th Street) at its website.

For the Archive House Gates and his crew salvaged materials from fire-damaged abandoned buildings in the neighborhood of Grand Crossing on Chicago's far south side. The artist replaces the typical aluminum siding with unpainted vertical boards reused from other structures and recycled windows of geometric rectangular and square shapes. The interior has plywood shelves and exposed wood stud construction for walls and the stair, with decorative plywood triangles at some walls. This object has none of the refined traditional craftsman ship of Edgar Miller's work but it has the rawness and expediency of unusual and textured materials that could be found in the early residential work of Frank Gehry.

For the Stony Island Bank building, purchased from the city for $1, the structure was renovated with the important decision to leave much of the decayed existing finishes alone. The plaster coffered ceiling of the main hall is fragmented and incomplete. This concept of leaving a historic structure in its dilapidated state instead of full period restoration was discussed as early as the 1970s when the stage director, Peter Brook, left the crumbling interior of the Bouffes du Nord theater in Paris to show its age and decrepitude. The poetry of the decay was evocative of the ghostly lives lived in these buildings so many years ago. The Chicago bank now is an arts center with libraries, changing gallery shows, installations and community art classes.

Lastly, I must briefly note the nearby "Reading Room" by Gates, which has part of its collection of (art installation?) 14,000 art and architecture books from the defunct Chicago landmark Prairie Avenue Bookstore. I was a patron of this bookstore for many years, first as a student and later as a visitor on holidays, and also sold a large chunk of my library back to the store as my limited shelf space became overpopulated. How strange to think that my own books (signature on first page) have traveled so far and changed so many hands to end up here waiting for another curious student to wander through their pages.

What could this possibly mean?

Stony Island Arts Bank Building (1923) - 6760 S. Stony Island Ave.
Architect: William Gibbons Uffendell - Interior Renovation (2015) - Artist: Theaster Gates

The Archive House
6900 block of South Dorchester
Renovation (2010)
Artist: Theaster Gates

CONCLUSION

KITSCH SOUVENIRS AND CHICAGO ARCHITECTURE

TRASH AND TREASURES

This essay is not about your Chicago Cubs key chain! It is however concerned with a topic few architects use but is still part of Architect-Speak that is the: *Objets à Réaction Poétique* and the *Objet Trouvé*, yes you guessed it, these are ideas that come from France.

For the most important and difficult French modern architect in the world, Le Corbusier (Charles-Édouard Jeanneret), gathering souvenirs on a 1950s summer Mediterranean beach holiday was not just a fun pastime but a serious aesthetic commitment. The items of his interest were nautilus shells, oyster shells, shapely rocks, twisted driftwood, spiky pine cones, bits of rope and best of all sliced bones from the local seaside restaurants. He labeled this collection as "Objects of a Poetic Reaction," he obsessively studied them and applied their unique shapes to many of his own paintings and building designs, which shows how architects can find influence and inspiration everywhere and from anything.

The second topic is titled "Found Objects" and is usually associated with the Surrealist writer and loud mouth: André Breton (and also Duchamp). He was the first to write about this condition in his 1937 prose poem, *Mad Love*. For him it was not the natural world's flotsam that was interesting but, instead, it was the urban culture of the Parisian flea markets with all their hallucinogenic historical bits of trash and memories. He also was searching for an object that spoke to him, not of curvy shapes but for the ultimate treasure, the twisted juxtaposition of elements that would produce a surrealist frisson. The American surrealist artist, Joseph Cornell, would be the best illustration of this collecting obsession for he would gather items to be placed in his discreet wooden box sculptures that would range from; plastic cubes, children's marbles, tiny aperitif glasses, faded photos of ballerinas, torn star charts, stained botanic prints, worn gambling dice, slot machine parts and movie star publicity shots. If you think about this list, it actually seems to have very consistent themes: discarded by the world, broken by sadness and lost in impossible love.

With those two concepts in mind, we can return to Chicago with all of its piles of souvenir crap and limit ourselves only to those objects that engage with the buildings of the city; which reduces the volume to a select number of items. The general topics would include, toy banks, charm bracelets, decorated ashtrays, Christmas ornaments, snow globes, tattered postcards and don't forget LEGO sets.

But I want to talk specifically about two items, one found on the cosmic flea market, the Internet, and the second would be the most famous of André Breton's "Found Objects" (or dream objects). Those would be my Skyline Key and Breton's *Slipper Spoon*.

SLIPPER SPOON

First to consider Breton's flea market find, a wooden spoon with an unusual bowl an interesting arc of a handle and a tiny carved woman's shoe at the end. To save time and oversimplify the analysis I will state my prejudice on what constitutes a surrealist object; it must address the topic of unifying sex and death. In most fairy tales a spoon is a feminine character and for this *Slipper Spoon* we can see the bowl, in its unusual teardrop shape, reinforcing that feminine idea with its form representing a vulva and the action of slurping from the spoon, a mimicking of cunnilingus. To top it off the tiny shoe at the handle's end is both hauntingly strange, a well-known fetish item and a perfect image of dismemberment. Therefore we have surrealistically united sex and death: *la petite mort*. Art history explained simply!

SKYLINE KEY

The second object is an enlarged metal key at about 8 inches long, probably a souvenir of the 1933 Chicago World's Exposition. The grooved teeth of the key's bit is a collection of three tiny stepped skyscrapers; the Medinah Athletic Club, the Civic Opera House and the Board of Trade, then proceeding up the object the shaft is the Chicago Theater's vertical sign gloomed on to an elongated Water Tower and the circular end (called the Bow) is what appears to be a collision of the Illinois state seal and domed State Capital. My interpretation of this unique object is that it is a perfectly metaphorical trope for this book: *Passe Partout*. For what is this publication but an attempt to give each reader a key to the city? It is a crude collage of monstrous skyscrapers reduced to microscopic size representations and in that transformation is another metaphor on how we understand those strange creatures. By writing a discrete summary of any of the towers I am shrinking them down to a size that the mind can easily encompass. It is possible to say that the microscopic and the macroscopic are consistent themes in surrealist art? Claude Lévi-Strauss talks about miniaturization in *The Savage Mind* (1962) and noted: "By being smaller, the object as a whole seems less formidable. By being quantitatively diminished, it seems to us quantitatively simplified."

Lastly, I must note the inclusion of two antique postcards from the author's collection: empty underground El train station and North Carcass Avenue. I find that both could simultaneously illustrate a moment in Chicago's history, a surrealist painting by Giorgio de Chirico and one of the lowest circles in Dante's *Inferno*.

The surrealist writer André Breton's wooden ladle with woman's shoe, *Slipper Spoon*, now at the Centre Pompidou, a found object from a Paris flea market in the 1930s.

A souvenir metal key to the city (1933) with its teeth as the urban skyline consisting of three specific towers: Medinah Athletic Club, Civic Opera House and Board of Trade Building. Its handle is the Chicago Sign, the Watertower and the Illinois State Capitol Dome at the end.

Skyline Key (1933) - author's collection

Historic postcard of Chicago with a surrealistic frisson, distorted one-point perspective of empty underground CTA train platform (1930) - metaphorically lost and hopeless in its emptiness.

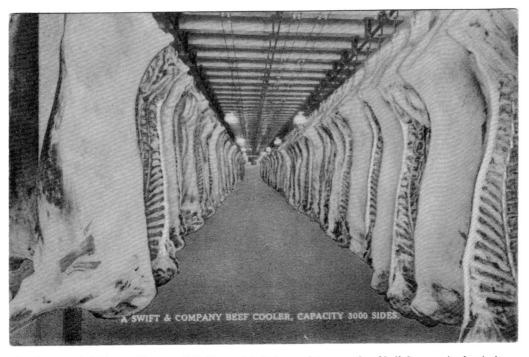

Historic postcard of Chicago with a surrealistic frisson, distorted one-point perspective of Swift Company beef cooler in Chicago Stock Yards (1920) - death as delight on N. Carcass Ave.

CHICAGO AS COLLAGE CITY

ROWE VS JENCKS

This is the dawning of a new age for architects to reinvent Chicago; no longer limited by the shackles of dogma and style they are now liberated to face every possible solution for sustainability, social change, design innovation and with that reality every possible confusion.

To end this journey down misanthropic memory lane I have first selected two education buildings that point to the conflicts of the current times and possible compromises to a probable vision of a new city made from many pieces of the old city. We will take another Architect-Speak phrase "Collage City," coming from the eponymous named book (1973) by design guru Colin Rowe and Fred Koetter, which seems pretty straightforward in that it describes that any new design must both fit in with the existing order and establish their own identity. To be both part of "tradition and utopia." How you connect to the old precedent is by playing the game of collage. Invented by Picasso and Braque around 1910 it consisted of gluing on canvas or paper various found material; music note sheets, wallpaper, newspaper, magazine adverts, cardboard, colored paper, on and on. For architects it is a phrase adapted to allow the combination of unlike things and ideas without anxiety. You make your design from components or memories of the wide world of art and architecture history.

For the second set of examples I will use two housing projects that layer on style and design literally one on top of another. This can best be related to the writings of that popinjay post modern architectural historian Charles Jencks in his book *Adhocism* (1972). Adhocism is an Architect-Speak word for the more familiar Claude Lévi-Strauss term in anthropology of *bricolage*. The difference between collage and *bricolage* is in the later's dramatic smashing together of different existing products that hobble together something new. On the cover of his book Jencks does his own *bricolage* by making a chair from bicycle handlebars, tractor seat and carriage wheels. Glaring contrasting differences are acceptable and encouraged. You make your design from what is on hand to use immediately and improvisationally.

COLLAGE CITY
McCORMICK TRIBUNE CAMPUS CENTER, IIT (2003)

This Illinois Institute of Technology student center is the result of a limited international architectural competition that enlisted some very famous designer names. It was won by the Rotterdam firm OMA and the globe trotting founding partner Rem Koolhaas, who presented a scheme that incorporated various existing structures as the El train tracks above, the existing Mies office designed Commons Building (1953) and the various diagonal pathways that student used traveling from their housing across to the main campus. The building is intentionally meant to stand out against the neutral black steel frame buildings of Mies and his followers by its facade being fluorescent orange! Each of the three items listed above were dramatically articulated in the new building. The screechingly loud El tracks were enclosed by a corrugated metal tube

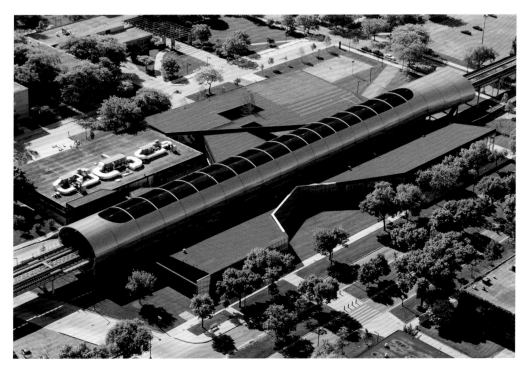

Aerial view - IIT - McCormick Tribune Campus Center (2003) - 3201 S. State St. - Architects: OMA - Rem Koolhaas

Entry facade and Mies portrait graphics (2x4 Inc.) - IIT - McCormick Tribune Campus Center (2003)

that visibly alters the roof line of the main building below it. The Commons building was connected with the most controversy as it was a historic modern building touched by the MASTER. So it was encircled with a triangular grass court at one point, covered with a cantilevered roof at the shared loading dock and just butted up against at the east facade. I could discuss other audacious innovations in the interiors , the surrealist contrast of adjacent functions (ping pong table at the main entry) or the lack of quality construction (Koolhaas has said "No money, no details") but for this essay the merging, both delicate and dumb, of the new building with the existing elements is the important point. I can't think of another building in Chicago that is so chock-a-block filled with ideas about how a building is added to the city in all its complexity and confusion. Perhaps the chapter title should have been, "Confusion City" (instead of the more political "Collusion City").

COLUMBIA COLLEGE MEDIA PRODUCTION CENTER (2010)

This is another low rise two-story education building that plays with ideas of collage; historic fragments, exposed program functions and technological imagery. The two buildings and courtyard, located in the South Loop, are designed by Studio Gang Architects and are a collection of soundstages, classrooms, digital labs and student center for photography and film production in the private school, Columbia College. The College has as its motto: *Esse Quam Videri*—"To be instead of appear," which is a bit of a contradiction for a film school that relies on pure cinematic and digital imagery. Perhaps a new maxim would be: *Tota Fallacia*—"All is an illusion."

The building is a most amazing assembly of architectural pieces some of those are organized in its wide open lobby: the terra cotta entry arch to a nearby demolished historic film warehouse "Famous Players Lasky Corporation" (forerunner to Paramount Pictures), a ceiling pattern of linear lobby lights that duplicate the radial TV test pattern graphic symbol, a monstrous colorful internally lit "Columbia" sign whose theme is extended into the glass facade with its irregularly placed colored glass panels (the custom font and signage is by Thirst and designer Rick Valicenti) and an over-scaled central stair that acts as movie seating for students to day-dream some future film. The new building is meant to be a shiny advertisement for the art and media school in contrast to the well-worn renovated masonry industrial buildings nearby (The terra cotta arch came about from the city's request that the college use it after the demolition of its building). It is a most loud and aggressive design which shouts at the passerby: "Hey you kid, why aren't you in this school to make that damn movie you've written?"

BRICOLAGE CITY
NORTHTOWN BRANCH LIBRARY (2019)

The Chicago Public Library, CHA and a private developer have established a program that integrates small centers of low-income senior public housing with updated branch libraries. For the Northtown location the architects, Perkins + Will, have gone for the adhocism solution of layering a completely different looking object

Columbia College Media
Production Center (2010)
1600 S. State St.
Architect: Studio Gang Architects

Lobby Interior - Columbia College
Media Production Center (2010)

on top of the library box. A precedent for this organization can be seen in Charles Jencks' Adhocism book in a fantasy drawing by architects Wimmenauer, Szabo, Kasper & Mayer that adds a glass tube structure over the Düsseldorf Art Academy in 1969. At Northtown the curvilinear double loaded corridor apartment block (44 units) does an S-shape twist to distinguish itself from the full perimeter library block below. For architects the twisted shape represents a modern "free form" that can be unregulated from any of the gridded constraints of the city. At the moment it is a wild anomaly in the neighborhood but perhaps an inspiration for similar changes.

Fantasy drawing of stacked tube structure over Düsseldorf Art Academy (1969)

STACKED HOUSING INFILL (2018)

This example is thrown in the mix of the other buildings to show that the author practices what he preaches. For an affordable housing competition, this fantasy solution was to take two existing townhouses with their adjacent abandoned and empty lots to establish a pattern of open and closed volumes repeated on the street, then to mimic that organization with a second set of new townhouse-like apartments at the fifth floor above the roofs of the present townhouses. A concrete frame structure with columns located in the empty lots provides the framework for the upper level housing with elevators and exit stairs at the rear sides. The entire low-rise, high-density assembly is quite surrealist in its appearance but references some famous housing with open cell yards by the French modern architect Le Corbusier. It is an example of the city made by a new adding layer on top of existing layer in another urban bricolage.

Stacked housing over library - Northtown Library (2019) - 6800 N. Western Ave. - Architect: Perkins + Will

Stacked Townhouses over Townhouses - Housing competition (2018) - Architect: Christian Bjone

Postcard: "Enchanted Island," a playground for children, Chicago World's Fair (1933)

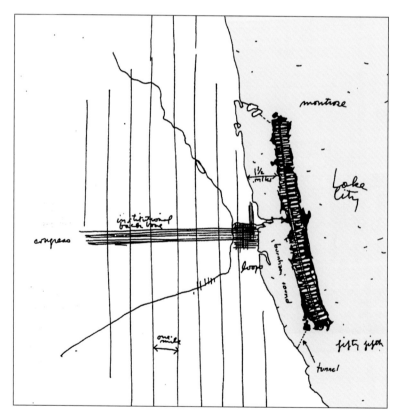

Lake City (1954) sketch by Harry Weese

Overleaf: Filter Island - Fantasy Project (2015) - Architects: UrbanLab

POSTSCRIPT

CHICAGO'S ENCHANTED ISLANDS

The lakefront is the defining edge to the City of Chicago, but its development is rather impoverished beyond beaches and marinas (and one amusement park). I have included here three fantasy proposals that show new islands off the coast line that might liberate both the spirit and the mind of the citizens and dreamers.

ENCHANTED ISLAND —1933 CHICAGO WORLD'S FAIR

The "Enchanted Island" was built in the 1933 Chicago World's Fair, A Century of Progress and was located at the area now labeled Northerly Island Park. It was basically an amusement park located out of the way of the serious exhibitions in the middle of the Fair. It has received little historical recognition, but I find it a fascinating design, almost a critical alternative to the City's grid. Its site plan has thin linear buildings creating shaped public spaces that circle around free-standing circular pavilions and articulated retail end pieces. Dramatic vertical electric signage columns establish a second grander scale along with the monstrous sized cut-out giraffes and elephants (designed by the artist Alfonso Iannelli). It is a pure surrealist spectacle but also an amazing urban design, much like St. Mark's Square in Venice, and much more complicated then the simple one-line circulation of the main section of the Fair. For entertainment it had a life-sized puppet theater, Coaster Wagon factory, house of marbles, mechanical zoo and a PIRATE SHIP!

LAKE CITY—1954 CHICAGO MAGAZINE

The architect Harry Weese was one of the unsung heroes of the post-war Chicago, whether it was in preservation (auditorium building), publications (*Inland Architect*), development (South Dearborne Street Lofts), or fantastic urban schemes. The proposal for an island city in Lake Michigan was part of a series of dreamscapes he did for *Chicago Magazine* in 1954. It was a ginormous island 15 miles long and 1.5 miles wide. It would have been insanely destructive in terms of noise, pollution and traffic congestion. It was both a transgressive innovation and a wrong-headed solution that is fortunately forgotten. Pretend I never mentioned it.

FILTER ISLAND—2015 CHICAGO BIENNIAL

The architecture firm UrbanLab founders Sarah Dunn and Martin Felsen have produced some of the most innovative and kooky designs for contemporary Chicago. Their hot fluorescent colored geometric fantasy for a new island in front of Grant Park, would have acted as both a public garden and an ecological filter for the periodic flooding of the Chicago River. No one assumes it would ever be built but its unironic audacity and its sincere aspirations are truly moving.

AUTHOR'S BIBLIOGRAPHY

ART AND ARCHITECTURAL HISTORY

Almost Nothing, 100 artists comment of the works of Mies van der Rohe, 2019

Philip Johnson and His Mischief, Appropriation in Art and Architecture, 2014

Art + Architecture, strategies in collaboration, 2009 (English and German editions)

First House, the grid, the figure and the void, 2002

FORTHCOMING

The Perfect Geometry of Death and Despair: Contemporary Artists Interpret Graves and Graveyards

Michelangelo in New York: Mannerist Influences in Modern Architecture

ILLUSTRATED CHILDREN'S BOOKS

The Very First Amazing Adventures of Griswold and Christophe, 2023

ACKNOWLEDGMENTS

The author would like to thank Linda Bjone, Robert Bruegmann, Stuart Cohen, Tom Nimen, Janet Parks and Kathryn Quinn for their thoughtful comments and review of the preliminary text.

And of course, thanks to Gordon Goff, Alejandro Guzman-Avila, Kirby Anderson and the editors and staff at ORO Editions.

PHOTO CREDITS

A TIMELINE OF CHICAGO'S ARCHITECTURAL HISTORY

1871 Mrs. O'Leary's cow kicks a lantern that starts a fire that nearly has the city kick the bucket

1889 Auditorium Building opens 4,237-seat theater with incredible acoustics by Adler and ornament by Sullivan

1892 Bronze Lions by Edward Kemey unveiled at the Palace of Fine Arts and later moved to the steps at the Art Institute of Chicago

1893 World's Columbian Exposition is held in Chicago in what is now Jackson Park on the South Side. This event starts the "City Beautiful" movement and the dominant neoclassical style in the States

1893 Public statue of *The Republic* by Daniel Chester French at Columbian Exposition, 1/3 size copy exists in Jackson Park

1896 Louis Sullivan's essay *The Tall Building Artistically Considered* first published

1909 Frank Lloyd Wright runs off with a client's wife to Europe and infamy

1910 Robie House completes the climax of Frank Lloyd Wright's Prairie Style

1912 Founding of the Burnham Library at the Art Institute of Chicago, later merged with Ryerson Library

1922 *Chicago Tribune Tower International Competition* awards first prize to Raymond Hood's Gothic pinnacle. The losers make history by inspiring designs built many years later

1924 Great architect Louis Sullivan dies an impoverished lonely old alcoholic in a dumpy hotel

1929 Stock Market Crash and Economic Depression. Chicagoans suffer till the start of WW2

1930 Ceres statue atop the Board of Trade building by John Storrs the visual climax to LaSalle Street by the city's best Art Deco tower

1933 Chicago World's Fair: A Century of Progress. An event immediately forgotten after its completion, with the exception of some modern houses by Keck & Keck

1938 Ludwig Mies van der Rohe finally leaves Nazi Berlin to escape to the warm embrace of a Chicago winter and a teaching position at the Armor Institute

1951 Mies designs glass towers; 860/880 North lake Shore Drive apartment buildings are opened. The best of his U.S. work and influential even today

1952 Carl Condit's book *The Rise of the Skyscraper: the Genius of Chicago Architects...*

1956 Graham Foundation is created with mission to fund architectural research

1964 City approves the 1948 commission on Lake Front Resolution, continuing the open, clear and free lakefront struggle

1965 UICC campus opens on the near west side, designed by SOM with Walter Netsch in charge, the zenith of the concrete brutalist style in Chicago

1965 The *Chicago Picasso* public sculpture and The Daley Center is opened, Architects: C.F. Murphy designed by Jacques Brownson and some say it is the best work from Miesian students

1968 City adopts Landmark Ordinance for Chicago Historical and Architectural Landmarks.

1969 John Hancock Skyscraper by SOM, super tall tower with Fazlur Khan Engineer and Bruce Graham as Partner. The skyline is changed forever

1972 Sullivan's masterpiece: the Chicago Stock Exchange is demolished and is the cause of death for the preservationist/photographer Richard Nickel. Stone arch and trading room are moved to the Art Institute

1976 Stanley Tigerman and Stuart Cohen organize a group of architects sarcastically self-labeled as the *Chicago Seven* to counter the idea of the city having only a structural based architectural tradition

1977 *Batcolumn* by Claes Oldenburg (101 foot tall) erected as city's first monumental pop art sculpture

1984 Chicago loses the title of the Second City when Los Angeles tries harder and Chicago becomes third in the total U.S. population

1985 Franz Schulze's book *Mies van der Rohe, A Critical Biography* published and revised in 2012

1991 Harold Washington Library Center completed by architect: Hammond Beeby and Babka, designer: Thomas Beeby, the peak of post modern style in the city

2003 McCormick Tribune Campus Center at IIT is opened, designed by OMA under Rem Koolhaas. The most dramatic structure in the deconstructionist style built in the city.

2004 Pritzker Music Pavilion designed by Frank Gehry is dedicated, an expressionist form that adds the Bilbao Effect for Chicago

2006 *Cloud Gate* public sculpture (the Bean) by Anish Kapoor with the completion of Millennium Park

2009 Aqua residential tower complete by Studio Gang. A new Sculptural Expressionism hits Chicago. Some say based on former employees of OMA and Rem Koolhaas

2009 Modern Wing at the Art Institute of Chicago opens designed by Renzo Piano and becomes the first international high tech design for the city

2014 George Lucas proposes his new Museum of Narrative Art on the lakefront by MAD architects, rejected by popular opinion, it is built in Los Angeles in 2023

2015 First *Chicago Architecture Biennial* to celebrate the city and the art of architecture worldwide

2016 Chicago becomes the "Murder Capital" of the U.S. (in total yearly murders) replacing the city of St. Louis, Missouri

2020 Apple Michigan Avenue store designed by Norman Foster becomes the city's second example of international high tech design. After the George Floyd protest riots and looting the store was damaged

MAPS

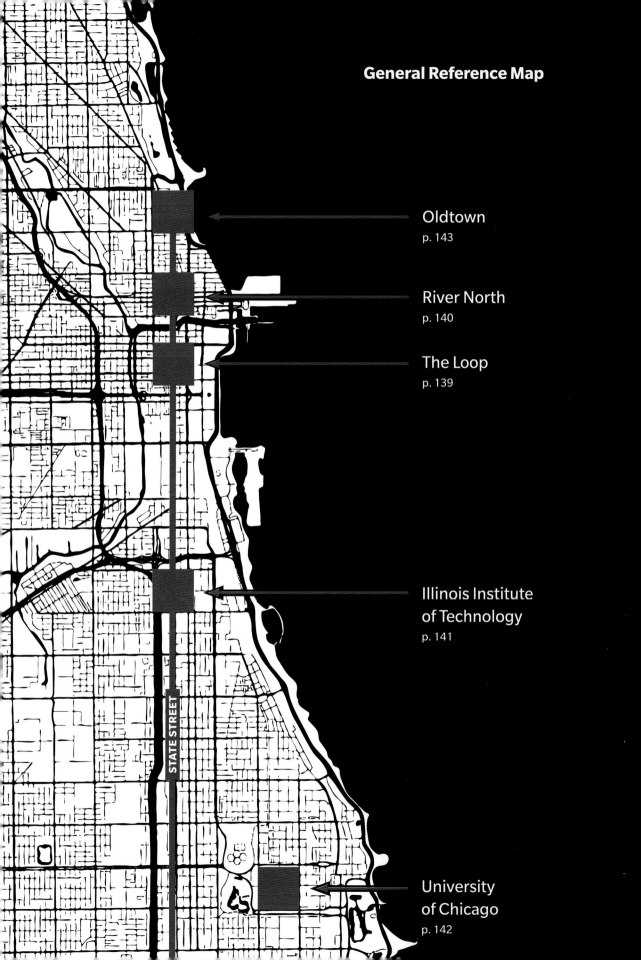

General Reference Map

Oldtown
p. 143

River North
p. 140

The Loop
p. 139

STATE STREET

Illinois Institute
of Technology
p. 141

University
of Chicago
p. 142

The Loop

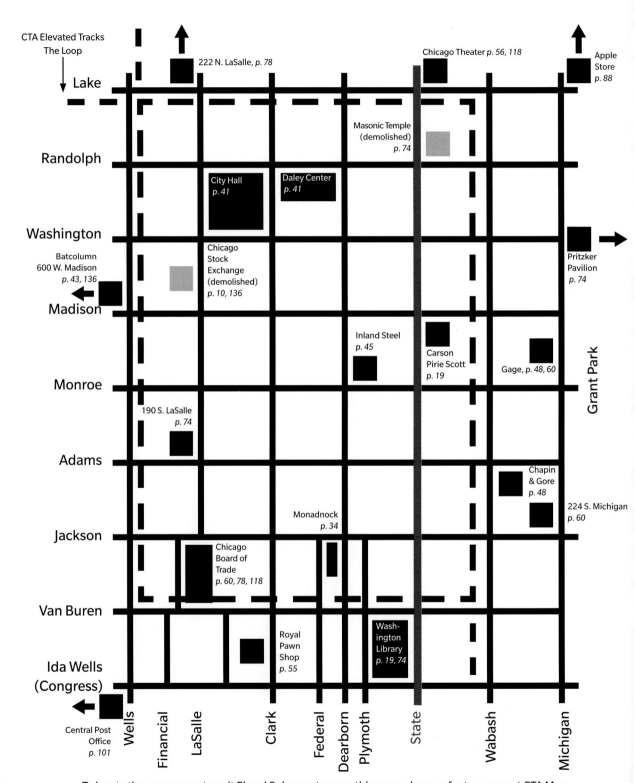

CTA Elevated Tracks
The Loop

222 N. LaSalle, *p. 78*

Chicago Theater *p. 56, 118*

Apple
Store
p. 88

Lake

Masonic Temple
(demolished)
p. 74

Randolph

City Hall
p. 41

Daley Center
p. 41

Washington

Batcolumn
600 W. Madison
p. 43, 136

Chicago
Stock
Exchange
(demolished)
p. 10, 136

Pritzker
Pavilion
p. 74

Madison

Inland Steel
p. 45

Carson
Pirie Scott
p. 19

Gage, *p. 48, 60*

Grant Park

Monroe

190 S. LaSalle
p. 74

Adams

Chapin
& Gore
p. 48

224 S. Michigan
p. 60

Monadnock
p. 34

Jackson

Chicago
Board of
Trade
p. 60, 78, 118

Van Buren

Royal
Pawn
Shop
p. 55

Wash-
ington
Library
p. 19, 74

**Ida Wells
(Congress)**

Central Post
Office
p. 101

Wells

Financial

LaSalle

Clark

Federal

Dearborn

Plymoth

State

Wabash

Michigan

To locate the many mass transit El and Subway stops on this map, please refer to a current CTA Map.

River North

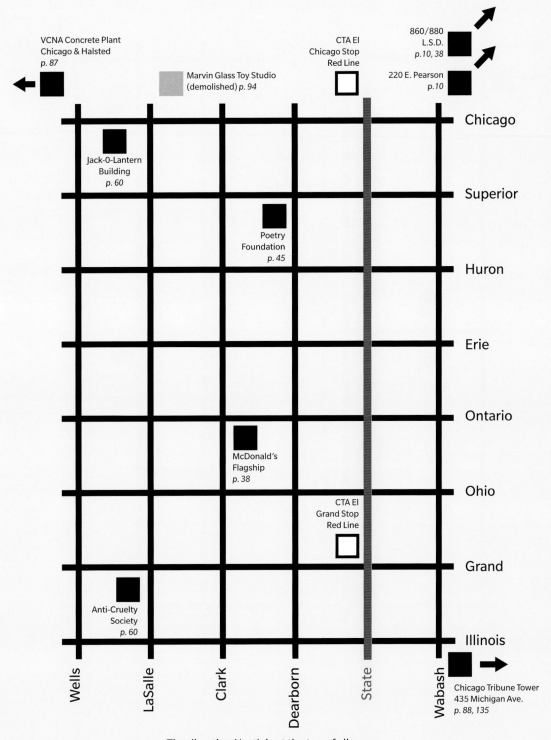

VCNA Concrete Plant
Chicago & Halsted
p. 87

Marvin Glass Toy Studio
(demolished) *p. 94*

CTA El
Chicago Stop
Red Line

860/880
L.S.D.
p.10, 38

220 E. Pearson
p.10

Chicago

Jack-O-Lantern
Building
p. 60

Superior

Poetry
Foundation
p. 45

Huron

Erie

Ontario

McDonald's
Flagship
p. 38

Ohio

CTA El
Grand Stop
Red Line

Grand

Anti-Cruelty
Society
p. 60

Illinois

Wells

LaSalle

Clark

Dearborn

State

Wabash

Chicago Tribune Tower
435 Michigan Ave.
p. 88, 135

The direction North is at the top of all maps.

Illinois Institute of Technology

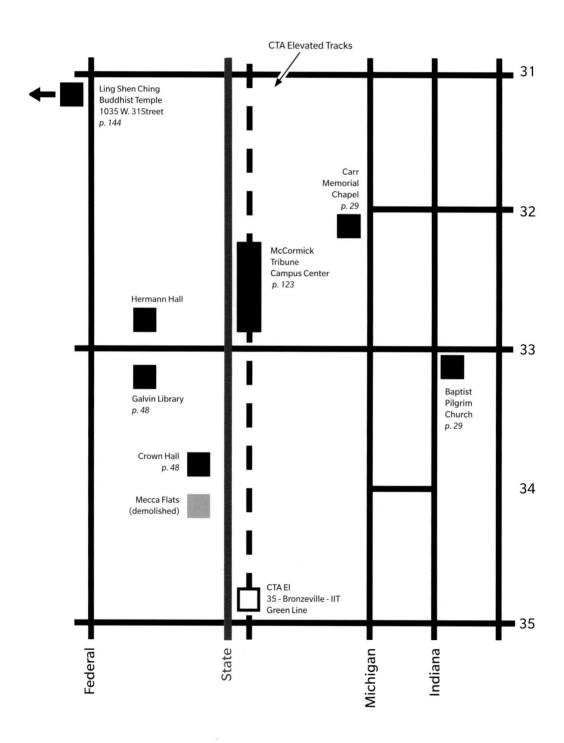

CTA Elevated Tracks

Ling Shen Ching
Buddhist Temple
1035 W. 31Street
p. 144

Carr
Memorial
Chapel
p. 29

McCormick
Tribune
Campus Center
p. 123

Hermann Hall

Galvin Library
p. 48

Baptist
Pilgrim
Church
p. 29

Crown Hall
p. 48

Mecca Flats
(demolished)

CTA El
35 - Bronzeville - IIT
Green Line

31

32

33

34

35

Federal

State

Michigan

Indiana

Not all buildings mentioned in the text are illustrated on these maps.

University of Chicago

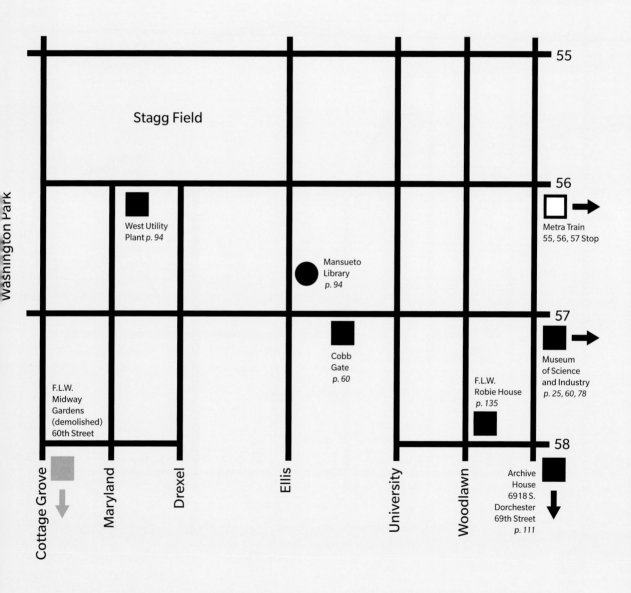

Washington Park

55

Stagg Field

56

West Utility
Plant *p. 94*

Metra Train
55, 56, 57 Stop

Mansueto
Library
p. 94

57

Cobb
Gate
p. 60

Museum
of Science
and Industry
p. 25, 60, 78

F.L.W.
Robie House
p. 135

F.L.W.
Midway
Gardens
(demolished)
60th Street

58

Archive
House
6918 S.
Dorchester
69th Street
p. 111

Cottage Grove

Maryland

Drexel

Ellis

University

Woodlawn

Please note that all maps are diagrammatic and not to scale.

Old Town

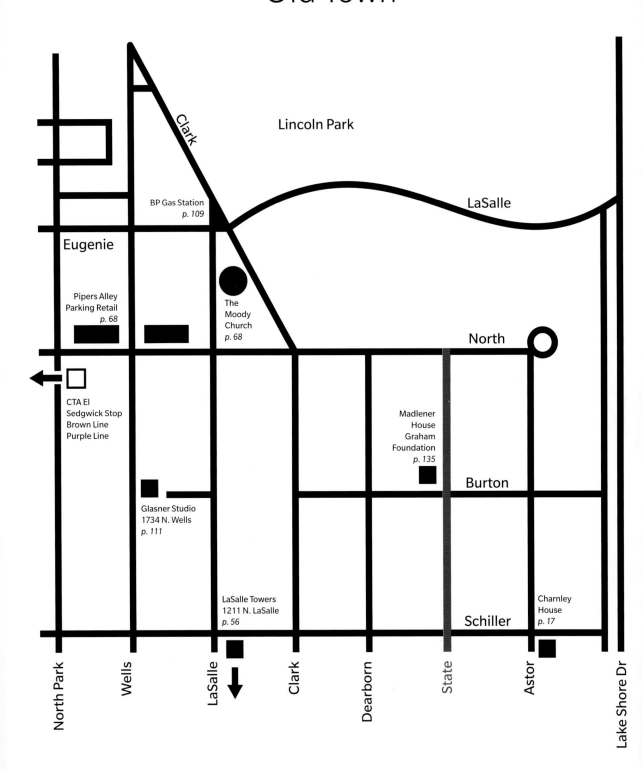

Lincoln Park

Clark

LaSalle

BP Gas Station
p. 109

Eugenie

Pipers Alley
Parking Retail
p. 68

The
Moody
Church
p. 68

North

CTA El
Sedgwick Stop
Brown Line
Purple Line

Madlener
House
Graham
Foundation
p. 135

Burton

Glasner Studio
1734 N. Wells
p. 111

LaSalle Towers
1211 N. LaSalle
p. 56

Schiller

Charnley
House
p. 17

North Park

Wells

LaSalle

Clark

Dearborn

State

Astor

Lake Shore Dr

The three houses represented here are open to the public by appointment.

PALIMPSEST

Ling Shen Ching Buddhist Temple (1892) -1035 W. 31 St. - originally Immanuel Presbyterian Church
Architect: Burnham & Root – Designer: John Wellborn Root.

A palimpsest is Architect-Speak for a building that shows the accumulation of additions and history on its facade. It is a medieval term for the precious paper that was scraped and erased so that it could be reused, but still shows the trace of the old text. Here the chinoiserie tile roof fragments are added on the unchanged arts and crafts masonry gabled facade. The rose window is covered with a mandala wheel while the cross at the roof peak is still visible. This is a dramatic example of the history of Chicago's buildings visible in all its layer after layer.

   The best possible example of how to end a book on Chicago's buildings: looking to both a future-perfect and a future on fire.

Yet on nights when, under all the arc-lamps,
the little men of the rain come running, you'll know
at last that, long long ago, something went wrong
between St. Columbanus and North Troy Street.
And Chicago divided your heart.

> *Leaving you loving the joint for keeps.*
> *Yet knowing it never can love you.*

— Nelson Algren (1951), *Chicago City on the Make*